DEALING WITH HUMAN RIGHTS

Asian and Western Views
on the Value of Human Rights

DEALING WITH HUMAN RIGHTS

Asian and Western Views on the Value of Human Rights

Edited by Martha Meijer

Greber
Publisher

WorldView
Publishing

Kumarian
Press

in association with
The Netherlands Humanist Committee on Human Rights (HOM)

Dealing with Human Rights: Asian and Western Views on the Value of Human Rights

© HOM, Utrecht, Netherlands 2001

This edition first published in 2001 by WorldView Publishing, 9 Park End Street, Oxford, OX1 1HH, United Kingdom (www.wvpub.com)

This edition published 2001 in North America by Kumarian Press, Inc., 1294 Blue Hills Avenue, Bloomfield, CT 06002, USA (www.kpbooks.com)

This edition published 2001 in the Netherlands and Belgium by Greber Publisher, Plantage Middenlaan 2L, 1018 DD Amsterdam, Netherlands. www.greber.nl (ISBN 90-5592-104-1)

First published as *Grondrecht en Wisselgeld: Aziatische en westerse visies op de waarde van de rechten van de mens* by Greber Publisher & Distributor.
Cover design by Nena Sesic-Fiser, *Night Cruising Flow Chart*, 1993
Translations from Dutch by Lee Mitzman © HOM, 2001

This publication is supported by the European Commission, Hivos (Humanist Institute for Development Cooperation) and NCDO (National Committee for International Cooperation and Sustainable Development).

The paper used in this publication meets the minimum requirements of both the American Standard for Information Science—Permanence of Paper for Printed Library Materials, ANSI Z39.48–1984 and the ISO 9706 standard for archival paper.

A catalogue record for this book is available from the British Library.
ISBN 1-872142-57-5 Cloth   ISBN 1-872142-58-3 Paper

Library of Congress Cataloguing in Publication data

> Grondrecht en wisselgeld. English
> > Dealing with human rights: Asian and Western views on the value of
> human rights / edited by Martha Meijer.
> > > > p.   cm.
> > Includes bibliographical references
> > ISBN 1-56549-128-9 (paper : alk. paper)
> > 1. Human rights. 2. Human rights—Cross-cultural studies. I. Meijer,
> Martha, 1946- II. Title.
> JC571 .G78324 2001
> 323—de21
> > > > > > > > 00-054973

Typeset by WorldView Publishing Services
Printed in the United Kingdom

Contents

Abbreviations

ACM	Adviescommissie Mensenrechten in het Buitenlands Beleid
	Advisory Committee on Human Rights in Dutch Foreign Policy
ANC	African National Congress
BMO	Breed Mensenrechten Overleg (Dutch human rights forum)
CESR	Centre for Economic and Social Rights
CFSP	Common Foreign and Security Policy
EC	European Community
EU	European Union
GATT	General Agreement on Tariffs and Trade
GONGO	Governmental non-governmental organization (designation in China to denote a pseudo-NGO)
HOM	Humanistisch Overleg Mensenrechten
	The Netherlands Humanist Committee on Human Rights
ICCPR	International Covenant on Civil and Political Rights
ICESCR	International Covenant on Economic, Social and Cultural Rights
ILO	International Labour Organization
INDOC	Indonesisch Documentatie en Informatiecentrum
	Indonesian Documentation and Information Centre
NGO	Non-governmental organization
NJCM	Nederlands Juristen Comité voor de Mensenrechten
	Dutch Committee of Legal Professionals for Human Rights
OECD	Organization for Economic Cooperation and Development
OSCE	Organization for Security and Cooperation in Europe
PAS	Partai Islam Sa-Malaysia (Islamic opposition party in Malaysia)
SER	Sociaal-Economische Raad
	Dutch Social-Economic Council
SIM	Studie- en Informatiecentrum Mensenrechten van de Universiteit Utrecht
	Utrecht University Human Rights Research and Information Centre
SIS	Sisters in Islam (Islamic women's movement in Malaysia)
SLORC	State Law and Order Restoration Council (Burma)
SM	Senior Minister
SOH	Stichting Oecumenische Hulp
	Foundation for Ecumenical Aid
UN	United Nations
UNESCO	United Nations Educational, Scientific and Cultural Organization
UDHR	Universal Declaration of Human Rights
WTO	World Trade Organization

INTRODUCTION

Martha Meijer

Some governments deny that human rights are universally applicable. Their chief arguments are that such rights conflict with their country's culture or impede economic development.

The fiftieth anniversary of the adoption of the Universal Declaration of Human Rights by the United Nations took place in 1998. Nevertheless, the declaration's application is far from universal.

Public debate is therefore necessary to explore the balance between the principal aspects of human rights, political power relationships and willingness to compromise. Conducting this discussion, however, requires some agreement on the universal validity of human rights.

This anthology contributes to the public debate about international human rights policy. In the Netherlands this debate began in 1995, especially following the statement by the then Minister of Foreign Affairs Hans van Mierlo in his memorandum to the Lower House *De herijking van het buitenlands beleid* (Redefining Foreign Policy)[1]: 'Several non-Western societies seek to emphasize their identity and cultural heritage. This applies to countries with a Confucianist as well as for those with an Islamic tradition. As a result, they resist concern for human rights as an effort motivated by specifically Western values. This clearly complicates promotion of human rights,' asserts Van Mierlo. He continues: 'The [Dutch] government wishes to highlight the universality of fundamental human rights. Cultural differences are no justification whatsoever for wrongdoings including – but not restricted to – torture.' This quote reflects the discussion's present impasse: respect for a people's own culture versus the emphasis on the universality of human rights.

Human rights observance has always been a subject of debate in international relations. During the Cold War several governments resisted all human rights interventions as infringements of their sovereignty, due to the ideological contradictions between East and West. They considered human rights to be an internal affair.

Since the end of the Cold War another argument has surfaced in the political debate about human rights. Some governments condemn intervention by other governments by invoking the inviolability of their own culture. In their view, human rights, as set out in the Universal Declaration, are at odds with their culture. This position fundamentally challenges the idea that human rights are universal.

The universality of human rights is based on the belief that everybody, all over the world, from the day he or she is born, is entitled to live in dignity, that states must guarantee this right, and that citizens deserve to be protected from government abuses of power. Human rights include the right to life, freedom from torture, freedom of expression and freedom of association. These and other rights are formulated and established in the Universal Declaration of Human Rights.

Human rights theories date back to when mankind began to form communities and states. On 10 December 1948 the member-states of the United Nations first adopted the Universal Declaration of Human Rights as a tangible document. Many human rights conventions have followed and are binding to the ratifying states. Nonetheless, governments often fail to observe the conventions.

All member-states of the United Nations officially reaffirmed the universality of human rights at the UN Human Rights Conference in Vienna in 1993. Governments thus have an obligation to uphold human rights beyond their own borders. They must also try to influence and improve each other's human rights situations, for example through diplomatic relations or trade agreements. To this end they use persuasion tactics and silent diplomacy or public condemnation and the imposition of sanctions. This pressure is part of negotiations and conditions. The interactions are no longer limited to individual governments; increasingly, economic power blocs are involved. Some governments assert that democratic freedoms impede their countries' economic growth: human rights versus market forces.

The effort to balance the principal aspects of human rights with political relationships and the willingness to compromise raises moral and political issues. Are governments entitled to impose conditions on each other's human rights policy? In which situations, and how can they do so most effectively? Are economic sanctions an appropriate instrument, and what is their scope? How can we activate a dialogue about the contrast between universality and upholding our own culture? In *Dealing with Human Rights*, four Asian and four Dutch authors address these questions.

The Contributors

Daan Bronkhorst, a publicist affiliated with the Dutch section of Amnesty International, describes the past and present significance of the Universal Declaration of Human Rights. He highlights the different cultural sources of inspiration in drafting the Declaration, ranging from Chinese to African philosophers. Bronkhorst also discusses the cultural-relativist criticism of the universality of human rights.

The Chinese philosopher and human rights activist *Xiaorong Li* analyzes the Asiatic values invoked in the debate about the universality of human rights. She then addresses what she perceives as a false contradiction between civil and political rights on the one hand and socio-economic rights on the other hand, as well as the false contradiction between the collective and the individual. She advocates including human rights in the public debate between citizens.

The political scientist and human rights activist *Farish A. Noor* introduces an Islamic view of human rights. He focuses on the book *Taj-us Salatin, Mahkota Segala Raja-Raja* (The Crown of Kings), published by the Muslim philosopher and scholar Buchara al-Jauhari on North Sumatra in 1603. Noor submits that everybody should devise a policy for guaranteeing human rights based on his or her cultural heritage. The West's political, economic and cultural dominance impedes this course of action.

In *Fareed Zakaria's* interview with Singapore's former Prime Minister *Lee Kuan Yew*, Lee explains the difference between the Western and Confucianist views of the relationship between the individual and the state and its consequences for the political systems and economic success of Asian countries. Some leaders use culture to deny the universal validity of human rights. Zakaria concludes the interview with a postscript in which he qualifies the contradiction between Western and Confucianist culture and sketches the political context.

Kim Dae Jung, a South Korean human rights activist and President of the Republic of Korea since early 1998, provides a response to Lee's statements. He submits that Asia has many democratic traditions and philosophies. Resistance by authoritarian political leaders is the biggest obstacle to the emergence of a democratic society. Kim supports the realization of a democratic system in Asian countries, where the Universal Declaration may serve as a source of inspiration and a cornerstone.

The conditionality of human rights in economic relations is the main theme of the chapter by *Willem van Genugten*, Professor of both International Law and Human Rights. He describes the conditions associated with human rights observance by the World Trade Organization (WTO) and the European Union. The more powerful states should be prevented from imposing conditions on other less powerful states at their discretion. The system is most effective when conditionality involves human rights in the economic sphere, such as labour conditions in a given country.

Hadewych Hazelzet, a researcher specializing in international political economy, examines ways to influence the human rights situation through economic restrictions. In discussing the principles of the Just Sanctions Doctrine she analyzes the moral considerations that come into play, analogous to the Just War Doctrine. She emphasizes the choice between responding to human rights violations and the possible consequences of economic sanctions for the lives of citizens.

Martha Meijer, Director of the Netherlands Humanist Committee on Human Rights, advances the idea of the human rights impact assessment. She presents this instrument as a method for evaluating the effectiveness of human rights interventions and urges an objective approach to decisions and arguments. In addition to reporting the human rights situation in their own country, states should report to each other on their interventions. Meijer advocates an accountable and consistent international policy.

The chapters in this anthology will stimulate the current human rights debate. The universal validity of human rights is beyond question.

Nonetheless, their universal application needs to be addressed over and over again. Stating these arguments explicitly and searching for areas of common ground and room for dialogue will further this process and will enable negotiations to establish acceptable conditions. It will also enhance our insight into the very essence of human rights.

NOTE

1. Lower House, The Netherlands, 24 337, No. 2, pp. 22-23.

Huig Bartels

Daan Bronkhorst graduated in sinology and philosophy and has been a staff member of the Dutch section of Amnesty International since 1979. He has written about human rights, refugees, and the work of non-governmental organizations for various organizations and publishers.

I

THE UNIVERSAL DECLARATION OF HUMAN RIGHTS

Origins, Significance, and Future

Daan Bronkhorst

Sources of Inspiration for Human Rights

Ancient Concepts

Human beings have contemplated human nature since the dawn of human civilization. Many have reflected upon mankind's intrinsic goodness or badness. Good human attributes were emphasized by traditions such as Christianity and by the Chinese Confucianist philosopher Mencius (Meng Tzu, third century BC). Other philosophers, for example Plato (fourth century BC) and his contemporary the Chinese legal philosopher Xun Zi, focused on the bad in mankind. These philosophers set great store by the enforcement of law and order, through dictatorial measures if necessary. Both types of philosophers formulated ideas about human rights principles, albeit from different perspectives.

In China, Mencius presented a great many ideas that were remarkably similar to the Western tradition of natural law.[1] Mencius submitted that mankind was naturally inclined to do good, to aspire to social conduct, harmony, and prudent actions. Is it not human nature to rescue a child about to fall into a well? This implies that rulers must cultivate what is intrinsically present in every human being. In war and economic crisis, people are unlikely to develop normal human nature; they can only become true human beings in conditions of peace, justice and harmony. Nor can human attributes be coerced, just as a plant cannot be induced to grow.

Mencius stated clearly that people have the right to resist tyrannical rulers: 'The people is of supreme importance... the ruler comes last... People who are subject to violence do not serve their rulers from the bottom of their heart but pay only lip service as long as they lack the strength to resist. People whose loyalty is earned through virtue will joyfully submit to the sovereign.' In 1911, the founders of the first Chinese republic quoted these words.

Islamic ideas about human rights stress that people are absolute equals, irrespective of race, religion, nationality or status.[2] According to the Holy Koran, no people or individual is superior to any other. Human beings are sacred and may not be killed, except after they have been tried in a court of law. Religion contains no coercive element, and the diversity of religions has been granted by God. Justice should always prevail over hatred. In addition, the Koran prescribes many duties. The more repressive views in some Islamic currents, such as those of fundamentalism, are based less on the Koran than on subsequent interpretations in the Shari'a (law).

A few sources were especially significant in the development of human rights ideas.[3] One was the Greek movement of Stoa philosophers. They considered mankind neither good nor evil; attributes were neutral and could be applied to good or bad ends. The Stoa also formulated far-reaching ideas about equality between people. The Greco-Roman philosopher Panaetius (second century BC) extended this equality to barbarians and slaves as well.

Natural law was another source. Greek philosophers from the fifth and fourth centuries BC distinguished *physis* (natural law) from *nomos* (law devised by human beings). Socrates, Plato and Aristotle claimed that fixed rules of law were identifiable as natural laws that transcend the laws devised by mankind. In the Middle Ages natural law was derived from the Bible. Thomas of Aquinas asserted that divine law, natural law and positive law should never conflict with one another. Hugo Grotius distinguished the moral standard from God or church and stated that set minimum standards were required for a stable society. This was where the idea originated for a social contract, which was elaborated from the seventeenth century. In 1776 the American Declaration of Independence turned natural law into a formulation of fundamental rights universally applicable to all individuals.

The concept of human dignity is another cornerstone of the human rights idea. That concept (Greek: *timè*; Latin: *dignitas*) did not apply to all people in equal measure. For example, dignity protected free citizens from torture and 'inhuman' types of executions, but did not cover slaves. The preambles to the Universal Declaration of Human Rights (1948) and the United Nations human rights conventions of 1966 mention the inherent dignity of members of the human family. The Universal Declaration further states that people should lead a dignified existence, and that all people merit the same dignity and rights.

Revolutionary Aspirations

Many human rights concepts originated in social revolutions.

The Magna Carta (or Great Charter) is viewed as the origin of the parliamentary system. In 1215 English barons issued this deed and had King John accede to it. The chief stipulations concerned the loan agreement between the king and the barons. Henceforth, special dues required approval from an assembly of barons, which later became the Parliament. A free Englishman could be imprisoned only after a verdict (unfree individuals lacked rights and were not covered by the Charter). If the king did not observe the stipulations, a committee of lords was entitled to instigate resistance. The Charter's immediate significance was minimal, since disputes between lords and kings would quickly recur. Nonetheless, the document was one of the first instruments restricting the king's virtually limitless power.

On 26 July 1581 the Acte van Verlatinghe (Secession Act) was signed in The Hague. In this document nine Dutch provinces denounced King Philip II of Spain. They explained that 'a sovereign is appointed by God to rule his people and to protect them from repression and violence the way a shepherd protects his flock of sheep...

When he stops doing this but represses them instead, he is no longer a ruler but a tyrant, and the people are entitled by law to elect another ruler.' The Act went down in history as one of the first official statements about the right to self-determination. The Act was examined by the Pilgrim Fathers, who had fled England in one of their first religious disputes and had sought refuge in Leiden for a while. They took the Act to America with them, where its spirit still resounds in the American Declaration of Independence.

During the Enlightenment – the philosophical and aesthetic movement that spread throughout Europe in the late seventeenth and early eighteenth centuries – various philosophers proposed that mankind was rational and could realize its potential without intervention by the church. The law had to be verified against reason and natural law. It was not 'conceived', but could be derived from natural laws through reason. Legal reform meant adapting old laws to the principles of rationality. This view influenced the constitutions of states such as Prussia, Austria and France.

On 4 July 1776 the American Declaration of Independence was adopted by the Continental Congress in Philadelphia. The declaration derived from natural law and affirmed the right of the settlers to end their ties with the British Crown, based on the fact that nobody had the right to rule without permission from the subjects. The first part of the declaration enumerates all the wrongful acts committed by the British Crown. Next comes a list of rights: all people are created equal and have an inalienable right to life, liberty and the pursuit of happiness. Governments exist by virtue of the people. The Declaration of Independence became an important source of inspiration to revolutionaries in Europe, especially in France, who viewed it as the realization of the ideals of the Enlightenment.

On 26 August 1789 the Assemblée Nationale in Paris adopted the French Declaration of the Rights of Man and of the Citizen. The preamble establishes the 'natural, inalienable and sacred rights of mankind'. Most of the seventeen chapters address civil and political rights and include such statements as that nothing may be forbidden unless it is prohibited by law; that nobody may be arrested arbitrarily; that individuals are to be presumed innocent until proven guilty; and that everyone has the right to freedom of conviction, religion and expression, as long as public order and laws are not violated.

International Law

The elaboration of human rights concepts into their present form is largely attributable to the proliferation of 'international law'. This term was first used by the British political philosopher Jeremy Bentham in 1780. The principle of legal provisions that transcend borders, however, dates back to Antiquity.

Ancient Jewish society distinguished between, on the one hand, tribes and communities that regarded each other as aliens but coexisted peacefully, and on the other hand, nations with which they had no relations and were engaged in warfare. The Greeks had forms of arbitration for conflicts between city-states. Philosophers such as Hugo Grotius turned ideas about natural law and the Roman *jus gentium* (law of the peoples) into the foundation of international law.

In the first half of the twentieth century the international community was concerned mainly with opportunities for keeping the peace, such as in the Peace Conferences in The Hague in 1899 and 1907. Enforcing the peace also became the principal mission of the League of Nations. This international organization was established in 1919, largely thanks to the efforts of US President Woodrow Wilson (1856-1924), whose own country never actually joined. In the 1930s the Soviet Union became a member, but Germany, Italy, Japan and other countries left the organization. The League of Nations was effective in keeping the peace on few occasions; it was, however, able to coordinate refugee relief, especially thanks to the efforts of Fridtjof Nansen (1861-1930) as High Commissioner of Refugees. Two independent organizations closely connected with the League of Nations were the Permanent Court of Arbitration and the International Labour Organization (ILO). The ILO pioneered the adoption of international human rights conventions. An ILO convention from 1930, for example, prohibits slavery and forced labour. Most international arrangements, however, such as those for refugees, were reached between separate countries and concerned only specific groups or circumstances. In other words, they were not universal.

World War II is considered a turning-point in the development of human rights for various reasons. First, widespread violence inflicted on citizens, for example through executions, hostage taking, bombings and reprisals, revealed the need to provide these people with better protection during wartime. This led to the 1949 Geneva Conventions on the protection of soldiers and civilians in war and armed conflict. Second, the Holocaust showed that 'civilized' peoples could commit horrible atrocities even toward members of their own population, and that minorities needed to be guaranteed protection against the government in their own country. This awareness led to standards of international human rights law within the UN, starting with the Universal Declaration of Human Rights. Third, the atomic bombs dropped on Japan in August 1945 revealed the power of such weapons and demonstrated the need for international agreements to control the arms race. The result was intensive negotiations about arms control and a series of treaties. Fourth, the trials in Nuremberg and Tokyo were the first manifestations of international justice dispensed by international courts, although they overlooked the war crimes committed by the Allies and the mass murders under Stalin in the Soviet Union. Since then, the Nuremberg Principles have been applied repeatedly in national trials, especially the one stipulating that a non-commissioned officer or official cannot be acquitted of crimes merely because he has received orders to commit them. Only in the 1990s were international tribunals established once again. In this case they dealt with crimes committed in the former Yugoslavia and Rwanda. Fifth, the huge post-war waves of refugees led to the first general Convention Relating to the Status of Refugees in 1951.

Foundations of the Universal Declaration of Human Rights

Origins

Many individuals helped draft the Universal Declaration. Among its authors, the French legal scholar René Cassin (1887-1976) deserves special mention. During World War II he was among those who devised international standards on genocide. He received the Nobel Peace Prize in 1968. The subtleties of the text, however, were not the work of only one man. They represented the collective effort of scholars, lawyers, politicians, and UN officials. Nor was the Declaration written exclusively by Western authors. Prominent members of the working group included specialists from Latin America and Asia.

Eleanor Roosevelt was the key figure in turning the Declaration into a political reality.[4] Her political involvement began as the wife of the American President Franklin Delano Roosevelt. After his death she became the chairwoman of the UN Commission on Human Rights in 1946. In her autobiography she describes the final stage as follows:

> *In the final vote in Committee Three, on presenting the Declaration to the Assembly, the delegates from four Moslem countries abstained, explaining that they believed the article on religious freedom was contrary to the Koran. We consulted Sir Zafrulla Khan, the foreign minister of Pakistan, the largest Moslem nation. 'It is my opinion,' he declared, 'that our Pakistan delegate has misinterpreted the Koran. I understand the Koran to say: He who cannot believe shall disbelieve; the only unforgivable sin is to be a hypocrite. I shall vote for acceptance of the Universal Declaration of Human Rights.'*
>
> *In the end there was no vote cast against the Declaration in the General Assembly, but there were some disappointing abstentions. The Soviet Union and its satellite countries abstained, since the Russian delegate contended that the Declaration put emphasis mainly on 'eighteenth-century rights' and not enough on economic, social and cultural rights. The delegate from Saudi Arabia abstained, saying he was quite sure King Ibn Saud would not agree to the interpretation of the Koran. South Africa also abstained, I was sad to note; its delegate said that they hoped to give their people basic human rights, but that the Declaration went too far.*

On 11 December 1948, a report by Reuters made the front page in newspapers all over the world:

> *The UN General Assembly has adopted the Declaration of Human Rights with 48 votes in favour, 0 opposed and 8 abstentions. The Soviet delegate Vishinsky had announced that the Soviet Union would not support the Declaration of Human Rights. 'It is an unacceptable intervention in the internal affairs of states,' explained Vishinsky. The Assembly rejected a Soviet proposal to defer the vote until the next year by 45 to 6 votes, with*

3 abstentions. Four Soviet amendments to the declaration were rejected as well. The Assembly applauded louder than at any other event during its three-month session when Eleanor Roosevelt was designated as the person who had done the most work for the Declaration of Human Rights. Previously, a spokesperson for the Slavic block had called her a tool of fascism. In the end, the Assembly adopted two resolutions requesting all governments to publicize the declaration as widely as possible and urging haste in establishing a human rights convention binding all states adopting it. The Declaration of Human Rights comprises thirty articles and is binding only in moral respects to the ratifying states.[5]

Types of Rights

Before we examine the text of the Universal Declaration and the resulting international law in more detail, we need to consider a few core concepts.[6]

First, what are 'rights'? Rights are primarily a legal concept, an advantage granted under a certain legal system. As a moral term, they refer to what is fair and just. Some authors distinguish between primary and secondary rights. Primary rights include 'good faith' rights, such as the enforcement of a contract, marital loyalty, safeguarding from injury, and protection of property. Secondary rights are associated with a legal instrument used in cases where the primary rights are not observed, such as the right to compensation for damages, dissolution of a marriage, and restitution of stolen property. Human rights were originally primary rights. Thanks to the legal protection included in international treaties, such as the right of victims of torture to compensation, they progressively came to resemble secondary rights.

Human rights comprise a number of categories. There is no agreement on their subdivisions, but the following is one of the more generally accepted classifications. First, there are the rights to life and inviolability of the person, also known as integrity rights. Second, there are civil and political rights, which include freedom of expression and assembly, the right to a public hearing by an impartial tribunal, and rights to take part in government and public activities. The first and second category together are often called the 'classical human rights', and some authors prefer to limit the concept of human rights *sensu strictu* to this set. The third category comprises social-economic rights, which guarantee a dignified material and spiritual existence for everybody. Finally, some regard collective rights as a fourth category of human rights. These are rights held by a people or community, such as the rights to peace, development and the use of natural resources.

Rights are inextricably linked with obligations. In law texts, obligations are defined as a legal disadvantage. They are what is due to another person, group or institution, or what has to be fulfilled as a condition for the enjoyment of a certain right. Obligations can be legal or extra-legal. Gratitude, for example, is an extra-legal obligation, while telling the truth is both a legal and an extra-legal obligation. Obligations cover various legal concepts, including liability, commitment and accountability. According to international human rights conventions, citizens may have obligations such as provision of public services in times of need and fulfilment of contracts.

Very few duties are stated implicitly or explicitly in the Universal Declaration, apart from the general obligation, of states and citizens alike, to promote and observe human rights. Article 29 refers to obligations in a very general manner: 'Everyone has duties to the community in which alone the free and full development of his personality is possible.' Nor do duties figure prominently in later human rights conventions. Only the African Charter on Human and People's Rights (1981) contains a more extensive list of obligations.[7]

Binding and Non-Binding International Law

The rights formulated in the various international declarations and conventions do not all have the same status and scope. The distinction between a declaration and a convention is especially important. A declaration is an official statement about certain rights and is not binding. A convention is a binding agreement between states. Designations such as act, agreement, charter, covenant, treaty and protocol are used – albeit somewhat inconsistently – for different types of conventions.

Principles that are included in a declaration may gradually acquire a binding effect. Adoption by many countries makes a declaration carry more weight. The principles may reach the status of 'customary law' if they are considered to be generally accepted rules of law. Some Third World countries have invoked customary law to legitimize the nationalization of natural resources. If other countries agree, customary law gradually becomes fixed, positive law. National courts often invoke international customary law as well. Some judges in the United States, for example, argue that youths under eighteen should not receive death sentences. This age limit figures in various conventions and is therefore considered to be accepted customary international law, even though the United States is not a party to the treaties containing this provision.

A remarkable aspect of human rights conventions, such as the 1966 International Covenant on Civil and Political Rights (ICCPR), is that certain rights are more 'binding' than others. They are known as non-derogable rights.[8] Such rights are never to be suspended, not even during war or a state of emergency. The status of rights labelled inalienable is less clear. The preamble to the ICCPR refers to the 'inalienable rights of all members of the human family [as] the foundation of freedom, justice and peace in the world'. This designation does not seem to add much substance: it seems to amount to little more than restating the fundamental and inherent character of human rights.

Somewhere between a non-binding declaration and a binding convention are codes of conduct. Sometimes they are merely advisory, while in other cases they are binding to certain sectors of society, such as companies or professional groups. The UN adopted a Code of Conduct for Law Enforcement Officials (1979) that prohibits torture and allows the use of firearms only in life-threatening situations. In 1979 the Parliamentary Assembly of the Council of Europe adopted a corresponding code for the police. The Principles of Medical Ethics, adopted by the UN in 1982, prohibit physicians and nurses from cooperating with torture in any way. In 1977 the European Community issued a code of conduct for firms with subsidiary operations in South Africa. Other codes of conduct for commercial corporations, which are by nature largely advisory, have been adopted by the International Labour Organization and the Organization for Economic Cooperation and Development (OECD).[9]

Finally, a fairly recent development in international law is the right to complain: the right to lodge a complaint or petition against human rights violations committed by a state. A state complaint concerns a complaint by one or more states against another state. Some conventions also allow individuals to lodge complaints against their own state. Generally, an international body will consider an individual complaint only after this individual has exhausted the judicial means in his or her own country. In particular, the individual right to petition as an 'option' to be adopted by parties to the European human rights system has proven an effective instrument.

The Text of the Universal Declaration

The Preamble

The preamble or introduction to the Universal Declaration elaborates on the considerations underlying the declaration. The wording of the preamble is grandiloquent: 'Whereas recognition of the inherent dignity and of the equal and inalienable rights of all members of the human family is the foundation of freedom, justice and peace in the world ...' and: 'Whereas disregard and contempt for human rights have resulted in barbarous acts which have outraged the conscience of mankind ...' Remarkably, this introduction does not mention a God or Supreme Being, as did its predecessors, the American Declaration of Independence and the French Declaration of 1789. While some delegates recommended including such references in the Universal Declaration, the final version does not.

Two phrases in the preamble are especially striking. First, the words 'if man is not to be compelled to have recourse, as a last resort, to rebellion against tyranny and oppression.' Here, the preamble is referring to the age-old customary right to rebel against a repressive regime or an unjust ruler – a concept already stressed by the ancient Chinese philosopher Mencius. Second, a sentence at the end of the preamble states that the Universal Declaration is proclaimed 'to the end that every individual and every organ of society, keeping this Declaration constantly in mind, shall strive by teaching and education to promote respect for these rights and freedoms.' Thus, the Universal Declaration addresses organizations and individuals as well as states. Human rights organizations have used this phrase to remind individuals and organizations, and especially commercial corporations, of their responsibilities for upholding human rights.

General and Integrity Rights

General and integrity rights are the most accepted concepts in human rights law and perhaps in the entire field of international law. Nearly everything on the subject in the Universal Declaration is also included in the two UN covenants of 1966 and in the regional human rights treaties of Europe, America and Africa. These rights include three non-derogable rights guaranteeing life, recognition as an individual before the law, and protection from torture. The general rights include the right to equality before the law, protection of privacy, and protection from discrimination.

Freedoms

The core freedoms comprise freedom of conscience, religion and thought; this right is non-derogable. The right to freedom of expression covers the right to gather, receive and transmit information and ideas, across borders and in whatever form. Legal restrictions may be imposed to protect the rights of others or the public order. Alternatively, enforcing other rights may lead to restrictions. Inciting racial violence, for example, is prohibited under the International Convention on the Elimination of All Forms of Racial Discrimination.

The right to association and assembly is another freedom right: people are free to associate and to join unions, barring restrictions such as those of the public order and others 'necessary in a democratic society'. Even in Western democracies, such restrictions have on occasion been imposed on the right to strike and the establishment of certain political parties (e.g. extremist ones).

Participation Rights

Participation rights concern the right to be part of a country's government or to hold public office, stand for election, and be involved in cultural events. The Universal Declaration mentions a few rights that subsequently recur in treaties, such as the right to vote and to be elected in general elections by secret vote, and equal rights to hold public office.

Other provisions include equal suffrage for men and women and the right to a nationality.

Rights of Arrested Persons, Defendants and Persons in Custody

The right to a fair trial is the most important among the rights of arrested persons, defendants and persons in custody. The Universal Declaration describes a few elements of these rights in general terms: freedom from arbitrary arrest, the right to a fair and public hearing by an independent and impartial tribunal, and the right to be presumed innocent until proven guilty. These details were elaborated in later conventions and declarations. The amendments include the right to a trial within a reasonable period, the means and time to prepare a defence, and the opportunity to appeal and to obtain clemency. Various subsequent declarations, such as the UN Standard Minimum Rules for the Treatment of Prisoners (1955), list extensive guidelines concerning clothing, food, medical care, etc.[10]

Rights of Vulnerable Groups

Protecting the rights of vulnerable groups is one of the least elaborate areas in the Universal Declaration. The declaration contains articles addressing equal rights for women and men and states that 'motherhood and childhood are entitled to special care and assistance'. The special rights that women, children, the elderly, minorities and other vulnerable groups deserve do not yet appear in the Universal Declaration. The Universal Declaration does, however, include the right to security during old age, a right that is not stated explicitly in a subsequent human rights treaty.

Rights of Aliens and Refugees

The Universal Declaration mentions the right to leave a country and to return to it, as well as the right to protection from *refoulement* (being returned to a country where one has a well-founded fear of persecution). These principles figure generally in human rights and refugee conventions. One clause in the Universal Declaration is unique: Article 14 mentions the right to 'seek and enjoy asylum'. The word 'enjoy' has been a subject of extensive discussions. None of the subsequent treaties stipulates that asylum seekers actually have the right to obtain asylum.

Social, Economic and Cultural Rights

Social and economic rights are rights to basic conditions of wellbeing and welfare. They appear in articles 22 through 26 of the Universal Declaration. These articles include approximately twenty different rights, including those regarding employment, remuneration, social security, education, housing, legal aid and medical care. The declaration also mentions rights to protection from unemployment, free and compulsory education, 'rest and leisure' and periodic holidays with pay.

Fundamental social rights were elaborated in the 1966 International Covenant on Economic, Social and Cultural Rights. Most of these fundamental rights contain formulations of conditions that should gradually materialize. Both outside and within the wealthy Western countries, many of these rights are clearly a long way off.

Cultural rights include the right to participate in cultural life and scientific progress, as well as copyright. They have been formulated as compulsory rights in subsequent treaties.

What is Missing

Although the Universal Declaration lists a very extensive series of rights, it has some shortcomings. For instance, it does not mention restrictions on the application of the death penalty, or the right to commutation of such a sentence. Other rights which cannot be found in the declaration include freedom of the press, freedom of scientific research, the right to strike, the right to use one's own language and name, and the individual right to complain. The declaration contains nothing about a prohibition on war propaganda or hate speech (i.e. encouragement of violence and discrimination). Protection of women (e.g. from genital mutilation) and children (e.g. from harmful work) was elaborated in international law only later.

Collective rights, such as those relating to the self-determination and development of peoples, are not mentioned either. This last point has elicited criticism among governments of Third World nations, many of which were not yet independent when the Universal Declaration was adopted.

An Ongoing Debate

Types of Critique

As we have seen, the Universal Declaration was already a subject of controversy upon its adoption in 1948. Twenty years later in 1968, the Proclamation of Tehran, adopted at the First UN World Conference on Human Rights, was an effort to update the Universal Declaration. Among the parties drafting this statement were many Third World nations that were not yet represented in the UN in 1948. This statement contains additional explicit references to issues such as apartheid, illiteracy, women's and children's rights, family planning and disarmament. This proclamation never received broad support and has been all but forgotten.[11]

In the run-up to the Second UN World Conference on Human Rights in 1993, a few governments (mostly from East Asian and Islamic states) called for a debate on the Universal Declaration's universal claims. But the World Conference culminated in a reaffirmation of this declaration. Nevertheless, a few of these governments later continued their efforts to revive the discussion.

What is the nature of the criticism against the Universal Declaration? There are two general types of criticism regarding the universal human rights claims: (a) theoretical, philosophical criticism and (b) criticism inspired largely by political and ideological motives. The following paragraphs list the keywords pertaining to the different types of criticism.

a) The *theoretical criticism* includes the following types.

Reactionary criticism. Since the end of the eighteenth century the idea of human rights has been challenged as a cover and an impediment for revolutionary changes that are needed. Human rights would only erode the social foundations without creating a new society that might guarantee a more humane existence.

Communist criticism. Ever since Karl Marx quoted Jeremy Bentham's aphorism that human rights are 'nonsense about nonsense, nonsense on stilts', radical socialism, Marxism, communism and Maoism have continuously expressed sharp criticism of the prevailing concept of human rights. Marxist principles formulate human rights largely in negative terms. According to the principle of class struggle, rights acquired by one class are always at the expense of another one. Human rights are interests acquired from the government by the bourgeoisie but simultaneously entail suppression of the interests of the working class. In revolutionary and communist societies the notion of human rights is superfluous, as the system of exploitation has made way for joint ownership of the means of production.

Communitarian criticism. Especially in the United States, a strong philosophical and ideological movement aims to curtail excessive liberalism of individual freedoms by invoking a sense of community and shared values.

Pragmatist criticism. A contemporary philosophical movement known as pragmatism aims to disengage as much as possible from values believed to derive from alleged natural law. Society is based at most on a temporary consensus, not on everlasting principles, and notions such as those of human rights are not inborn or 'inherent' to mankind.

b) Most of the *politically and ideologically motivated criticism* comes from the governments of Third World countries. The politically motivated criticism comprises the following categories.

Socialist criticism from the centrally planned economies, a modernized and diluted form of the communist criticism described above.

'Confucianist' criticism, which comes largely from governments in East Asia: the Universal Declaration does not give adequate consideration to the stability a society acquires through its traditional relationships (ruler-subject, parents-children, old-young) and through its emphasis on the community over the individual.

'African' criticism: the prevailing view of human rights does not give adequate consideration to specific conditions from the colonial past, miserable living conditions, international exploitation, and traditional relationships of communities and tribes in Africa.

Religious-fundamentalist criticism (of which the criticism from Islamic fundamentalism is the most explicit): the Universal Declaration does not acknowledge that rights are granted by God, and that they must be observed according to His principles and those of prophets and religious authorities.

'Unaligned' criticism: from Indonesia to Brazil and from India to Kenya, governments have stated that traditional forms of law, reconciliation and conflict control are more appropriate and more effective than internationally imposed standards.

These critical perspectives enable a summary of the main issues of doubt raised with respect to the Universal Declaration's universal claims and the arguments against them along four general lines.

A. Internal Cohesion of the Universal Declaration

Is this declaration a faithful and consistent account of the main principles of international law, or are some elements rather arbitrary and possibly contradictions of other elements? Is the Universal Declaration based on an unambiguous principle (in natural law), or is it more an enumeration of positive legal principles?

Analysis of the text reveals that the Universal Declaration is not intended as a logical and philosophically consistent text. The Universal Declaration is indeed an enumeration. Some rights are absent but appear later in other declarations, and the Universal Declaration also lists rights not covered extensively in international law.

Most of the Universal Declaration's content, however, is confirmed in subsequent binding treaties. In this manner the Universal Declaration has proven its value as a cornerstone in constructing the framework of human rights. The conventions are widely accepted in most cases, even by countries that have criticized the Universal Declaration.

B. Interpretations of the Universal Declaration

Are stipulations such as the right to life, a dignified existence, and protection of integrity and basic needs subject to interpretation so as to suggest a list of intentions or principles rather than of rights?

The relatively brief text of the Universal Declaration, which identified a great many rights, was too short for precise definitions. Definitions of most of these rights appear in later conventions and declarations, which addressed selected rights. In the corresponding UN convention, for example, torture is defined as:

Any act by which severe pain or suffering, whether physical or mental, is intentionally inflicted on a person for such purposes as obtaining from him or a third person information or a confession, punishing him for an act he or a third person has committed or is suspected of having committed or intimidating or coercing him or a third person or for any reason based on discrimination of any kind when such pain or suffering is inflicted by or at the instigation of or with the consent or acquiescence of a public official or other person acting in an official capacity. It does not include pain or suffering arising only from, inherent in or incidental to lawful sanctions.

Many of the terms listed in the Universal Declaration have thus become genuine rights that provide a basis for clearly described claims. Moreover, every law or definition of rights is subject to a degree of interpretation – as is the case in the everyday practice of national justice systems.

C. Cultural Context of the Universal Declaration

Does the context reflect rights and principles pertaining largely to Western historical trends, and of little or no significance in non-Western religions and political traditions?

This category of criticism is known as 'cultural relativism'. It refers to the idea that certain practices are considered violations in some cultures but not in others. Examples include circumcision of women (clitoridectomy), burning of widows, the death penalty, or forms of corporal punishment.

Cultural relativism has been with us for a long time. The French philosopher Pascal (1623-1662) wrote: 'Truth on this side of the Pyrenees is untruth on the other side.' In 1947, while the Universal Declaration was being drafted, the American Anthropological Association issued the following statement: 'Only when a statement of the rights of men to live in terms of their own traditions is incorporated into the proposed Declaration, then can the next step of defining the rights and duties of human groups as regards each other be set upon the firm foundation of the present-day scientific knowledge of Man.'

Such sweeping relativism raises objections for several reasons. First, it is unclear what this 'scientific knowledge of Man' entails. Does scholarly research reveal that cultures are very different, or are they essentially derived from the same choices and patterns? Our limited knowledge of the diversity of cultures suggests that standards are indeed largely universal. All cultures have principles such as the fundamental obligation to tell the truth, the prohibition of murder and theft, and the protection of the vulnerable from the whims of rulers.

Second, cultural relativism can easily lead to arbitrariness. Appreciating another culture is impossible unless one takes a stand.

Third, the relative differences have only dwindled from the perspective of international development. International mutual dependence (interdependence) and the need to preserve the peace between peoples and states command consideration for the respective cultures as well as for the rules that are now commonplace throughout the international community. The rising standards of international conventions render references to cultural relativism progressively less convincing. At the beginning of the twentieth century, for example, corporal punishment was an accepted practice in most countries in the world. Today, it occurs in only a minority of states.

Various human rights experts have tried to distinguish between justified relativism and universal standards. Determining whether certain customs, such as circumcision of women or corporal punishment, are exempt from universal standards requires examining aspects such as their proliferation, their acceptance by the local population, or the government's inability to discontinue them. Other factors include the degree to which certain rights are considered non-derogable, absolute or inalienable. Protection from torture and slavery, for example, figures prominently in international law. Any practice with the slightest trace of torture or slavery merits highly critical scrutiny.

The status of the different rights provides a guideline for the discussion as to whether or not there is a hierarchy of human rights. Several declarations, including the one from the UN World Conference on Human Rights in Vienna (1993), have emphasized that all human rights are 'indivisible and interdependent'. The right to freedom from torture is not intrinsically superior to the right to employment or rest. Nevertheless, the various rights require different efforts for their implementation. While the right to employment or a decent standard of living cannot be imposed by governments at their discretion, protection from torture or arbitrary execution can. Human rights are not hierarchical in substance, but efforts and pressure to protect the different rights conform to a sequence of priorities.

D. Sustainability of the Universal Declaration

Has the Universal Declaration become obsolete, for example because of the subsequent emergence of post-colonial societies, the new international order, the globalization of the economy and communications, or the appeal for self-determination for peoples and cultural groups?

As noted, the proposals to amend the Universal Declaration (e.g. to include collective rights, such as those to development and peace) have yet to be reflected in binding treaties. They are regarded with suspicion by democratic governments and human rights experts alike. Collective rights may stretch the concept of human rights too much. If a 'people' obtains the same claim to rights as an individual, collective rights will be more likely to clash with individual human rights.[12] It is often unclear which parties will be responsible for enforcing these collective rights, or who requires protection from violations of them. Many collective rights pertain more to the law of nations than to human rights law. The international order that is best for certain peoples or communities is generally easier to achieve through negotiations than by invoking the alleged 'fixed' rights.

Present-day Application of the Universal Declaration

Justice and Democracy

Justice exists in social, political, moral, legal and other forms. It serves as a guideline for formulating and interpreting laws. For example, legislation does not generally prescribe fixed sentences for certain offences. Such a practice would be unjust, as it would preclude considering circumstances, capacity and shared guilt. Justice may also be accomplished extra-judicially, for example through reconciliation. The

Universal Declaration offers such guidelines but does not associate them with specific measures or sanctions.

Many constitutions, including those of the Netherlands and Belgium, list civil rights. In the French constitution, however, they are virtually overlooked, while the United Kingdom does not even have a constitution. A constitution or list of civil rights is not necessary to guarantee a just society.

Democracy is a different matter. Explicitly and implicitly, democracy is a core concept in human rights treaties today. The stipulations on freedom in human rights theory may be realized only through a form of democracy that presumes freedom of expression, the right to participate in public administration, elections by a secret vote and the granting of rights to minorities. In this respect, the Universal Declaration is a blueprint for democracy.

The declaration also presumes citizenship for all individuals. Only in the last hundred years, with the introduction of women's suffrage, have virtually all adult inhabitants of democratic states become citizens. Limited citizenship is possible without having the nationality of one's country of residence, as in the Netherlands, where foreigners have the right to vote in municipal elections under certain conditions.

Individual vs. Communitarian

Do rights clash with community spirit? The two different views are known as liberal and communitarian. According to the liberal perspective, protection of rights is the most important foundation for an honest, democratic community. The communitarian view submits that excessive emphasis on rights leads to selfishness and pursuit of self-interest, and that a community can function only if people are willing to waive their rights for the general benefit.

This debate is highly topical and relevant, as many matters presently being discussed in Western democracies demonstrate. For example, should certain rights of criminal suspects be attributed less importance in a war on crime, so as to avert endless appeals against sentences or the release of dangerous individuals? Should protection of the environment take precedence over personal enrichment that leads to excessive consumption? Is subordination of the individual rights of culture, tradition and language necessary for the integration of residents of foreign derivation and minorities?

The Universal Declaration accommodates both the liberal and the communitarian views. It presumes protection of civil rights but also emphasizes the right 'to a social and international order in which the rights and freedoms set forth in this Declaration can be fully realized'. The relative importance of these rights can be determined through deliberations, negotiations and jurisprudence.

Life and Integrity

The Universal Declaration states that every human being has the right to life but does not define when life begins, although proposals to this effect were made in the preparatory discussions. Many believe that the formula permits the death penalty. Death penalty opponents, however, argue that this exceptionally cruel punishment certainly violates the right to freedom from torture and cruel treatment if not the right to life. Arbitrary killing is clearly prohibited under the terms of the Universal Declaration, and practices such as wholesale political killings and genocide (murder of an ethnic group) are prohibited under separate conventions or under provisions regarding crimes against humanity.

A few international conventions have been amended to include optional protocols urging abolition of the death penalty: the European Convention on the Protection of Human Rights and Fundamental Freedoms, the American Convention on Human Rights, and the ICCPR. These protocols either prohibit the death penalty entirely or subject its application to conditions. Since the Universal Declaration's adoption, international law is clearly moving toward abolishing the death penalty.

Laws imposing corporal punishment have virtually disappeared from many Western nations but persist in others. Even some respected human rights activists have defended corporal punishment – including amputation – as an alternative to the inhuman prison conditions in those countries.[13] Other activists view life imprisonment (even in decent prisons) as a form of torture. The advanced standards regarding the prohibition of torture and cruel treatment appear to provide grounds for rejecting all forms of corporal punishment just as they do for rejecting the death penalty.

Freedom from Discrimination

The Universal Declaration states that all people are born free and equal in dignity and rights. Discrimination literally means 'distinction'. The concept's original significance was neutral, and has remained so in its scientific usage, for example in experimental psychology. In practice, however, the term has also acquired a negative connotation and has come to be associated with negative distinction and neglect. The prohibition of such negative forms of discrimination is one of the core concepts in human rights. The Universal Declaration and human rights conventions prohibit discrimination on grounds such as birth, skin colour, language, race, personal conviction, religion and belief, gender, social origin, and status. Special conventions address racial discrimination and discriminating practices against women.

The Universal Declaration's general message is that individual attributes that are not an individual's choice (e.g. colour and sex), or which pertain to peacefully practised convictions and beliefs, should never be cause for disadvantage. This element in the Universal Declaration is probably the most widely propagated and the most convincing. In this sense, the Universal Declaration is a blueprint for a multicultural society.

Non-discrimination prescribes the right to equal treatment: equality in situations such as access to work, remuneration, recognition of status for women, ethnic minorities, homosexuals, and others. Equality is the right to equal access but not to equal returns. The distribution of commodities and privileges depends in part on efforts, natural talents and the like. The UN covenants of 1966 prescribe equal treatment. The stipulations, however, leave the discussion about specific measures unresolved. Questions such as whether equal treatment is compatible with positive discrimination or whether registration of minorities is necessary to ensure equal treatment demand striking a balance between applicable human rights standards. In such areas, human rights law functions vertically as well as horizontally: fundamental rights not only apply in relationships between authorities and subjects, but also between individual citizens. For example, a refusal by confessional school boards to hire homosexual teachers presented as the right to choose a school according to one's own religious views can be challenged on the ground that it conflicts with the fundamental right to freedom from discrimination.

Intervention

The legal validity of collective rights, such as those to peace, development and a clean environment, remains a subject of debate. One topical issue has become prominent in the debate about 'humanitarian intervention' (i.e. the use of armed force by a state or states against another one to end massive human rights violations). Can such intervention be based on the right to peace or to self-determination of peoples, or should it be regarded solely as a means to stop violations of 'classical' rights? Chapter VII of the United Nations Charter provides for intervention to protect international peace. In such cases the affected population's right to humanitarian assistance might serve as a standard. It does not seem necessary to label this right to assistance a particular collective right. It may be derived from provisions in international declarations and conventions stipulating rights to life, freedom from torture and an adequate standard of living.[14]

Recently, the human rights debate has started to explore the application of another form of intervention: that of bringing to justice perpetrators of war crimes, crimes against humanity, and genocide, if necessary even outside the country where they have been committed. The crucial question is how the validity of international standards can be translated into laws, legal procedures and tribunals. Are these tribunals 'victors' justice', or are they the beginning of a new legal order? In the last years of the twentieth century, international opinion clearly favoured the second view. In June 1998 the UN adopted the statute for a permanent International Criminal Court. In October of that year, the arrest of former Chilean head of state General Pinochet was widely welcomed as the first important example of the realization of 'universal jurisdiction'.

Some progress has also been made in determining the extent to which the international community should waive prosecution for the sake of national reconciliation and keeping the peace. The UN Charter calls for conciliation during conflicts between states, while the Geneva

Protocols of 1977 (amendments to the Geneva Conventions of 1949) call for the 'widest possible' amnesty after an armed conflict. Official 'truth and reconciliation' commissions, such as in Chile and South Africa, maintained that granting amnesty or waiving prosecution may be justified, provided such action does not compromise the search for the truth and acknowledgement of responsibilities. Human rights organizations such as Amnesty International, however, continue to argue that amnesty can be granted only after the outcome of a trial. Neither the Universal Declaration nor other declarations and conventions as yet provide a clear foundation for either position.[15]

The Future of the Universal Declaration

What lies in store for human rights law and the awareness of human rights? How will the future of the Universal Declaration be affected? There are three current trends.

The first trend is that of broader applicability and greater specificity. The principles of human rights and their legal application are being amended constantly, both internationally and within states. Since the Universal Declaration's adoption, a great many conventions and declarations have been established and ratified by an ever-growing number of states. New conventions and declarations are under development or subject to debate. The conceptual scope of human rights has broadened. Other proposals urge extending human rights law to cover the environment and sustainable development, cultural assets, animals, outer space, and any extraterrestrial life as well. This expansion coincides with elaboration; the definitions of the various human rights are becoming more specific and more detailed.

In this process, the Universal Declaration's significance does not appear to be diminishing. It remains the standard for an impressive list of core rights, which may remain the foundations of international and national law for a long time to come.

The second trend is the growth in means for improving human rights observance. Intergovernmental facilities now include commissions, Special Rapporteurs, working groups, monitoring operations, and more. Opportunities for the right to counsel (as in the 'consultative status' of NGOs) and the complaint right of states, individuals and organizations are growing as well. International human rights operations are becoming increasingly important: peacekeeping missions, humanitarian interventions, monitoring of elections, restoration after war. Recently, the international justice system established a permanent international criminal court. Official human rights institutions have proliferated in many countries. They include commissions for truth and reconciliation, ombudsmen, special prosecutors and national commissions or advisory councils for human rights. International and national non-governmental human rights organizations have contributed substantially. The international ones are expanding their scope and operations; the largest, Amnesty International, now has over a million members worldwide and sections in about sixty countries. In recent years the number of local independent human rights organizations has also grown rapidly.

On their own, the stipulations in the Universal Declaration are not a broad enough basis for developing new measures. New rules and provisions will need to be established to anticipate situations that were not an issue when the Universal Declaration was adopted. On the other hand, increasing the focus on the Universal Declaration in this situation of strong growth seems a positive strategy. After all, the Universal Declaration is the most widely accepted foundation and can ensure consistency to avert arbitrariness. Nowadays, the mandate of intergovernmental operations often includes a reference to the Universal Declaration. Non-governmental organizations also refer to the Universal Declaration in their mandates and working rules and are encouraging others to do so as well, for example by urging commercial corporations to include the Universal Declaration in their business principles. By basing their work on the Universal Declaration, organizations that defend certain rights or protect the interests of specific groups express their support for the indivisibility of human rights. In other words, they are affirming the need to extend the rights they are claiming for certain groups to all other groups as well. Such a statement of principles ensures that the objectives and means of organizations do not become increasingly particularist.

The third trend is the heightened awareness of the foundations underlying our actions as moral, socially functional human individuals. In this area, the language of rights has its limitations.

After all, our daily life is not always determined by awareness of our rights. We are guided in equal measure by feelings and emotions, by hope and worries. The Universal Declaration fails to mention love, desire, compassion, or solidarity. Nor does it refer to fear, hatred, vengeance, or remorse. The Universal Declaration neither prohibits deceit or greed, fails to encourage tenderness or warmth toward others, nor entitles people to concern or forgiveness. Do these aspects of life exceed the scope of rights and their declarations? Can they be addressed only in the worlds of religion and philosophy, or in exemplary individuals of exceptional moral standing or in role models presented by television soap series?

In his essays about human rights, the French philosopher Emmanuel Levinas has attempted to bridge the gap between the lofty ideals of human rights and the moral demands of ordinary life.[16] He wrote about the need to relieve the denial of others; about individual responsibility as the foundation for all freedom; about the 'small goodness' perceptible among people, even among those with ample reason to hate each other; about the obligation to consider people not only objectively, for example according to their rights, but also subjectively, according to what they aim to be and to express; and about the prophetic character of human rights activists, without whom civilization would never have made any progress.

If a clearer link emerges between the rights of the Universal Declaration and the emotions of our ordinary life, the essential significance of rights will prevail, and human rights observance will become more likely.

The text of the Universal Declaration of Human Rights (UDHR) is included as an appendix to this book.

NOTES

1. Arthur Waley (1939). *Three Ways of Thought in Ancient China*. London: Allen and Unwin. For a modern Chinese interpretation of human rights based also on Confucianist concepts, see Jacqueline Smith, Ed. (1996). *Human Rights: Chinese and Dutch Perspectives*. The Hague: Martinus Nijhoff Publishers.
2. Abdullahi Ahmed An-Na'im *et al.* (1995). *Human Rights and Religious Values: An Uneasy Relationship?* Amsterdam: Rodopi.

3. Unfortunately, no general account of the history of human rights concepts and activism is available at this time. A summary appears in Hillary Poole, Ed. (1999). *Human Rights: The Essential Reference.* Phoenix: Oryx Press.

4. Eleanor Roosevelt (1961). *The Autobiography of Eleanor Roosevelt.* New York: Harper. For the history of the Universal Declaration, see Åshild, Samnøy (1993). *Human Rights as International Consensus: The Making of the Universal Declaration of Human Rights, 1945-1948.* Bergen, Norway: Chr. Michelsen Institute. See also Paul Gordon Lauren (1998). *The Evolution of International Human Rights: Visions Seen.* Philadelphia: University of Pennsylvania Press and Johannes Morsink (1999). *The Universal Declaration of Human Rights. Origins, Drafting, and Intent.* Philadelphia: University of Pennsylvania Press.

5. As quoted in the Dutch daily *Het Parool,* 11 December 1948.

6. For an overview of human rights issues, see e.g. Theodor Meron, Ed. (1985). *Human Rights in International Law: Legal and Policy Issues.* Oxford: Clarendon Press.

7. For a compendium of human rights law, see Philip Alston, Ed. (1996). *Human Rights Law.* New York: New York University Press.

8. In the ICCPR, the non-derogable rights are the right to life; freedom of conscience and belief; recognition as a person before the law; freedom from torture and cruel treatment; protection from detention for debts; protection from being punished twice for the same crime.

9. For an overview of human rights and business, see Daan Bronkhorst and Gemma Crijns (2000). *Corporate Approaches: Human Rights and Business.* Amsterdam: Amnesty International (unpublished).

10. Nigel S. Rodley (1985, 1999 2nd edn.). *The Treatment of Prisoners in International Law.* Oxford: Clarendon Press; New York: Oxford University Press.

11. See B.G. Ramcharan, Ed. (1979). *Human Rights: Thirty Years after the Universal Declaration: Commemorative Volume on the Occasion of the Thirtieth Anniversary of the Universal Declaration of Human Rights.* The Hague: Martinus Nijhoff. See also: SIM Special No. 9 (1989). *The Universal Declaration of Human Rights: Its Significance in 1988.* Utrecht: Netherlands Institute of Human Rights (Studie en Informatiecentrum Mensenrechten); Peter R. Baehr (1999). *Universality in Practice.* New York: St. Martin's Press.

12. For a defence of collective rights as human rights, see e.g. Nico Schrijver (1997). *Sovereignty over Natural Resources: Balancing Rights and Duties.* New York: Cambridge University Press. For the argument that collective rights contradict human rights, see Rhoda Howard, 'Dignity, Community and Human Rights', in John Witte and Johan D. van der Vyver, Eds. (1996c). *Religious Human Rights in Global Perspective: Legal Perspectives.* The Hague: Martinus Nijhoff.

13. As is argued by Abdullahi Ahmed An-Na'im in his chapter 'Towards a Cross-Cultural Approach to Defining International Standards of Human Rights', in Abdullahi Ahmed An-Na'im, Ed. (1992). *Human Rights in Cross-Cultural Perspectives: A Quest for Consensus.* Philadelphia: University of Pennsylvania Press.

14. As is argued in Dutch Interchurch Aid (1992). *Protocol on the Right to Humanitarian Assistance.* Utrecht: Stichting Oecumenische Hulp.

15. Daan Bronkhorst (1995). *Truth and Reconciliation: Obstacles and Opportunities for Human Rights.* Amsterdam: Amnesty International. See also Priscilla B. Hayner (2000). *Unspeakable Truths: Confronting State Terror and Atrocities.* New York: Routledge.
16. Colin Davis (1997). *Levinas: An Introduction.* Notre Dame, IN: University of Notre Dame Press.

Ellen Verwiel

Xiaorong Li studied Philosophy at the Universities of Sichuan and Wuhan in China, earned her Ph.D. in philosophy from Stanford University, USA and was assistant professor at the People's University in Beijing. Now she is a research scholar at the Institute for Philosophy and Public Policy at the University of Maryland, USA. Li is vice-chair of the organisation Human Rights in China. From 1990 to 1992 she was the editor of the journal *Human Rights Tribune*. In her research and publications Li has focused on ethical and political issues at an international level.

2

'ASIAN VALUES' AND THE UNIVERSALITY OF HUMAN RIGHTS

Xiaorong Li

Orientalist scholars in the nineteenth century perceived Asians as the mysterious and backward people of the Far East. Ironically, as this century draws to a close, leaders of prosperous and entrepreneurial East and Southeast Asian countries eagerly stress Asia's incommensurable differences from the West and demand special treatment of their human rights record by the international community. They reject outright the globalization of human rights and claim that Asia has a unique set of values, which, as Singapore's ambassador to the United Nations has urged, provide the basis for Asia's different understanding of human rights and justify the 'exceptional' handling of rights by Asian governments.[1]

Is this assertion of 'Asian values' simply a cloak for arrogant regimes whose newly gained confidence from rapidly growing economic power makes them all the more resistant to outside criticism? Does it have any intellectual substance? What challenges has the 'Asian values' debate posed to a human rights movement committed to globalism?

Though scholars have explored the understanding of human rights in various Asian contexts, the assertion of 'Asian values' gains political prominence only when it is articulated in government rhetoric and official statements. In asserting these values, leaders from the region find that they have a convenient tool to silence internal criticism and to fan anti-Western nationalist sentiments. At the same time, the concept is welcomed by cultural relativists, cultural supremacists, and isolationists alike, as fresh evidence for their various positions against a political liberalism that defends universal human rights and democracy. Thus, the 'Asian values' debate provides an occasion to reinvigorate deliberation about the foundations of human rights, the sources of political legitimacy, and the relation between modernity and cultural identity.

This essay makes a preliminary attempt to identify the myths, misconceptions, and fallacies that have gone into creating an 'Asian view' of human rights. By sorting out the various threads in the notions of 'cultural specificity' and 'universality', it shows that the claim to 'Asian values' hardly constitutes a serious threat to the universal validity of human rights.

Defining the 'Asian View'

To speak of an 'Asian view' of human rights that has supposedly emanated from Asian perspectives or values is itself problematic: it is impossible to defend the 'Asianness' of this view and its legitimacy in representing Asian culture(s). 'Asia' in our ordinary language designates large geographic areas which house diverse political entities (states) and their people, with drastically different cultures and religions, and unevenly developed (or undeveloped) economies and political systems. Those who assert commonly shared 'Asian values' cannot reconcile their claims with the immense diversity of Asia – a heterogeneity that extends to its people, their social-political practices and ethnic-cultural identities. Nonetheless, official statements by governments in the region typically make the following claims about the so-called 'Asian view' of human rights:

- Rights are 'culturally specific';
- The community takes precedence over individuals;
- Social and economic rights take precedence over civil and political rights;
- Rights are a matter of national sovereignty.

Claim I: Rights are 'culturally specific'

Human rights emerge in the context of particular social, economic, cultural and political conditions. The circumstances that prompted the institutionalization of human rights in the West do not exist in Asia. China's 1991 White Paper[2] stated that 'owing to tremendous differences in historical background, social system, cultural tradition and economic development, countries differ in their understanding and practise of human rights.' In the Bangkok Governmental Declaration, endorsed at the 1993 Asian regional preparatory meeting for the Vienna World Conference on Human Rights, governments agreed that human rights 'must be considered in the context of a dynamic and evolving process of international norm-setting, bearing in mind the significance of national and regional peculiarities and various historical, cultural, and religious backgrounds.'[3]

Claim II: The community takes precedence over individuals

The importance of the community in Asian culture is incompatible with the primacy of the individual, upon which the Western notion of human rights rests. The relationship between individuals and communities constitutes the key difference between Asian and Western cultural 'values'. An official statement of the Singapore government, *Shared Values* (1991), stated that 'an emphasis on the community has been a key survival value for Singapore'. Human rights and the rule of law, according to the 'Asian view', are individualistic by nature and hence destructive of Asia's social mechanism. Increasing rates of violent crime, family breakdown, homelessness, and drug abuse are cited as evidence that Western individualism (particularly the American variety) has failed.

Claim III: Social and economic rights take precedence over civil and political rights

Asian societies rank social and economic rights and 'the right to economic development' over individuals' political and civil rights. The Chinese White Paper (1991)[4] stated that 'to eat their fill and dress warmly were the fundamental demands of the Chinese people who had long suffered cold and hunger.' Political and civil rights, according to this view, do not make sense to poor and illiterate multitudes; such rights are not meaningful under destitute and unstable conditions. The right of workers to form independent unions, for example, is not as urgent as stability and efficient production. Implicit here is the promise that once people's basic needs are met – once they are adequately fed, clothed, and educated – and the social order is stable, the luxury of civil and political rights will be extended to them. In the meantime, economic development will be achieved more efficiently if the leaders are authorized to restrict individuals' political and civil rights for the sake of political stability.

Claim IV: Rights are a matter of national sovereignty

The right of a nation to self-determination includes a government's domestic jurisdiction over human rights. Human rights are internal affairs, not to be interfered with by foreign states or multinational agencies. In its 1991 White Paper[5], China stated that 'the issue of human rights falls by and large within the sovereignty of each state.' In 1995, the government confirmed its opposition to 'some countries' hegemonic acts of using a double standard for the human rights of other countries . . . and imposing their own pattern on others, or interfering in the internal affairs of other countries by using "human rights" as a pretext.'[6] The West's attempt to apply universal standards of human rights to developing countries is disguised cultural imperialism and an attempt to obstruct their development.

Elsewhere and Here

In this essay I address the first three claims that make up the 'Asian view', particularly the argument that rights are 'culturally specific'. This argument implies that social norms originating in other cultures should not be adopted in Asian culture. But, in practice, advocates of the 'Asian view' often do not consistently adhere to this rule. Leaders from the region pick and choose freely from other cultures, adopting whatever is in their political interest. They seem to have no qualms about embracing such things as capitalist markets and consumerist culture. What troubles them about the concept of human rights, then, turns out to have little to do with its Western cultural origin.

In any case, there are no grounds for believing that norms originating *elsewhere* should be inherently unsuitable for solving problems *here*. Such a belief commits the 'genetic fallacy', in that it assumes that a norm is suitable only to the culture of its origin. But the origin of an idea in one culture does not entail its unsuitability to another culture. If, for example, there are good reasons for protecting the free expression of Asian people, free expression should be respected, no matter whether the idea of free expression originated in the West or Asia, or how long it has been a viable idea. And in fact, Asian countries may have now entered into historical circumstances where the affirmation and protection of human rights is not only possible but desirable.

In some contemporary Asian societies, we find economic, social, cultural, and political conditions that foster demands for human rights as the norm-setting criteria for the treatment of individual persons and the communities they form. National aggregate growth and distribution, often under the control of authoritarian governments, have not benefited individuals from vulnerable social groups – including workers, women, children, and indigenous or minority populations. Social and economic disparities are rapidly expanding. Newly introduced market forces, in the absence of rights protection and the rule of law, have further exploited and disadvantaged these groups and created anxiety even among more privileged sectors – professionals and business owners, as well as foreign corporations – in places where corruption, disrespect for property rights and arbitrary rule are the norm. Political dissidents, intellectuals and opposition groups who dare to challenge the system face persecution. Meanwhile, with the expansion of communications technology and improvements in literacy, information about repression and injustice has become more accessible both within and beyond previously isolated communities; it is increasingly known that the notion of universal rights has been embraced by people in many Latin American, African, and some East and Southeast Asian countries (Japan, South Korea, Taiwan, and the Philippines). Finally, the international human rights movement has developed robust non-Western notions of human rights, including economic, social, and cultural rights, providing individuals in Asia with powerful tools to fight against poverty, corruption, military repression, discrimination, cultural and community destruction, as well as social, ethnic, and religious violence. Together, these new circumstances make human rights relevant and implementable in Asian societies.

Culture, Community, and the State

The second claim, that Asians value community over individuality, obscures more than it reveals about community, its relations to the state and individuals, and the conditions congenial to its flourishing. The so-called Asian value of 'community harmony' is used as an illustration of 'cultural' differences between Asian and Western societies, in order to show that the idea of individuals' inalienable rights does not suit Asian societies. This 'Asian communitarianism' is a direct challenge to what is perceived as the essence of human rights, i.e., its individual-centred approach, and it suggests that Asia's community-centred approach is superior.

However, the 'Asian view' creates confusions by collapsing 'community' into the state and the state into the (current) regime. When equations are drawn between community, the state and the regime, any criticisms of the regime become crimes against the nation-state, the community and the people. The 'Asian view' relies on such a conceptual manoeuvre to dismiss individual rights that conflict with the regime's interest, allowing the condemnation of individual rights as anti-communal, destructive of social harmony, and seditionist against the sovereign state.

At the same time, this view denies the existence of conflicting interests between the state (understood as a political entity) and communities (understood as voluntary, civil associations) in Asian societies. What begins as an endorsement of the value of community and social harmony ends in an assertion of the supreme status of the regime and its leaders. Such a regime is capable of dissolving any non-governmental organizations it dislikes in the name of 'community interest', often citing traditional Confucian values of social harmony to defend restrictions on the right to free association and expression, and thus wields ever more pervasive control over unorganized individual workers and dissenters. A Confucian communitarian, however, would find that the bleak, homogeneous society that these governments try to shape through draconian practices – criminal prosecutions for 'counterrevolutionary activities', administrative detention, censorship, and military curfew – has little in common with his/her ideal of social harmony.

Contrary to the 'Asian view', individual freedom is not intrinsically opposed to and destructive of community. Free association, free expression, and tolerance are vital to the wellbeing of communities. Through open public deliberations, marginalized and vulnerable social groups can voice their concerns and expose the discrimination and unfair treatment they encounter. In a liberal democratic society, which is mocked and denounced by some Asian leaders for its individualist excess, a degree of separation between the state and civil society provides a public space for the flourishing of communities.

A False Dilemma

The third claim of the 'Asian view', that economic development rights have a priority over political and civil rights, supposes that the starving and illiterate masses have to choose between starvation and oppression. It then concludes that 'a full belly' would no doubt be the natural choice. Setting aside the paternalism of this assumption, the question arises of whether the apparent trade-off – freedom in exchange for food – actually brings an end to deprivation, and whether people must in fact choose between these two miserable states of affairs.

When it is authoritarian regime leaders who pose this dilemma, one should be particularly suspicious. The oppressors, after all, are well-positioned to amass wealth for themselves, and their declared project of enabling people to 'get rich' may increase the disparity between the haves and the have-nots. Moreover, the most immediate victims of oppression – those subjected to imprisonment or torture – are often those who have spoken out against the errors or the incompetence of authorities who have failed to alleviate deprivation, or who in fact have made it worse. The sad truth is that an authoritarian regime can practise political repression and starve the poor at the same time. Conversely, an end to oppression often means the alleviation of poverty – as when, to borrow Amartya Sen's example, accountable governments manage to avert famine by heeding the warnings of a free press.[7]

One assumption behind this false dilemma is that 'the right to development' is a state's sovereign right and that it is one and the same as the 'social-economic rights' assigned to individuals under international covenants. But the right of individuals and communities to participate in and enjoy the fruit of economic development should not be identified with the right of nation-states to pursue national pro-development policies, even if such policies set the stage for individual citizens to exercise their economic rights. Even when 'the right to development' is understood as a sovereign state right, as is sometimes implied in the international politics of development, it belongs to a separate and distinct realm from that of 'social-economic rights'.

The distinction between economic rights and the state's right to development goes beyond the issue of who holds these particular rights. National development is an altogether different matter from securing the economic rights of vulnerable members of society. National economic growth does not guarantee that basic subsistence for the poor will be secured. While the right to development (narrowly understood) enables the nation-state as a unit to grow economically, social-economic rights are concerned with empowering the poor and vulnerable, preventing their marginalization and exploitation, and securing their basic subsistence. What the right of development, when asserted by an authoritarian state, tends to disregard, but what social-economic rights aspire to protect, is fair economic equality or social equity. Unfortunately, Asia's development programmes have not particularly enabled the poor and vulnerable to control their basic livelihood, especially where development is narrowly understood as the creation of markets and measured by national aggregate growth rates.

A more plausible argument for ranking social and economic rights above political and civil rights is that poor and illiterate people cannot really exercise their civil-political rights. Yet the poor and illiterate may benefit from civil and political freedom by speaking, without fear, of their discontent. Meanwhile, as we have seen, political repression does not guarantee better living conditions and education for the poor and illiterate. The leaders who are in a position to encroach upon citizens' rights to express political opinions will also be beyond reproach and accountability for failures to protect citizens' social-economic rights.

Political-civil rights and social-economic-cultural rights are in many ways indivisible. Each is indispensable for the effective exercise of the other. If citizens' civil-political rights are unprotected, their opportunities to 'get rich' can be taken away just as arbitrarily as they are bestowed; if citizens have no real opportunity to exercise their social-economic rights, their rights to political participation and free expression will be severely undermined. For centuries, poverty has stripped away the human dignity of Asia's poor masses, making them vulnerable to violations of their cultural and civil-political rights. Today, a free press and the rule of law are likely to enhance Asians' economic opportunity. Political-civil rights are not a mere luxury of rich nations, as some Asian leaders have told their people, but a safety net for marginalized and vulnerable people in dramatically changing Asian societies.

Universality Unbroken

The threat posed by 'Asian values' to the universality of human rights seems ominous. If Asian cultural relativism prevails, there can be no universal standards to adjudicate between competing conceptions of human rights. But one may pause and ask whether the 'Asian values' debate has created any really troubling threat to universal human rights – that is, serious enough to justify the alarm that it has touched off.

The answer, I argue, depends on how one understands the concepts of universality and cultural specificity. In essence, there are three ways in which a value can be universal or culturally specific. First, these terms may refer to the *origin* of a value. In this sense, they represent a claim about whether a value has developed only within specific cultures, or whether it has arisen within the basic ideas of every culture.

No one on either side of the 'Asian values' debate thinks that human rights are universal with respect to their origin. It is accepted that the idea of human rights originated in Western traditions. The universalist does not disagree with the cultural relativist on this point – though they would disagree about its significance – and it is not in this sense that human rights are understood as having universality.

Second, a value may be culturally specific or universal with respect to its prospects for *effective (immediate) implementation*. That is, a value may find favourable conditions for its implementation only within certain cultures, or it may find such conditions everywhere in the world.

Now, I don't think that the universalist would insist that human rights can be immediately or effectively implemented in all societies, given their vastly different conditions. No one imagines that human rights will be fully protected in societies that are ravaged by violent conflict or warfare; where political power is so unevenly distributed that the ruling forces can crush any opposition; where social mobility is impossible, and people segregated by class, caste system, or cultural taboos are isolated and uninformed; where most people are on the verge of starvation and where survival is the pressing concern. The list could go on. As we shall see, however, to acknowledge that the prospects for effective implementation of human rights differ according to circumstances is not to legitimize violations under these unfavourable conditions, nor is it to deny the universal applicability or validity of human rights (as defined below) to all human beings no matter what circumstances they face.

Third, a value may be understood as culturally specific by people who think it is *valid* only within certain cultures. According to this understanding, a value can be explained or defended only by appealing to assumptions already accepted by a given culture; in cultures that do not share these assumptions, the validity of such a value will become questionable. Since there are few universally shared cultural assumptions that can be invoked in defence of the concept of human rights, the universal validity of human rights is problematic.

The proponents of this view suppose that the validity of human rights can only be assessed in an intracultural conversation where certain beliefs or assumptions are commonly shared and not open to scrutiny. However, an intercultural conversation about the validity of human rights is now taking place among people with different cultural assumptions; it is a conversation that proceeds by opening those assumptions to reflection and re-examination. Its participants begin with some minimal shared beliefs: for example, that genocide, slavery, and racism are wrong. They accept some basic rules of argumentation to reveal hidden presuppositions, disclose inconsistencies between ideas, clarify conceptual ambiguity and confusions, and expose conclusions based on insufficient evidence and oversimplified generalizations. In such a conversation based on public reasoning, people may come to agree on a greater range of issues than seemed possible when they began. They may revise or reinterpret their old beliefs. The plausibility of such a conversation suggests a way of establishing universal validity: that is, by referring to public reason in defence of a particular conception or value.

If the concept of human rights can survive the scrutiny of public reason in such a cross-cultural conversation, its universal validity will be confirmed. An idea that has survived the test of rigorous scrutiny will be reasonable or valid not just within the boundaries of particular cultures, but reasonable in a non-relativistic fashion. The deliberation and public reasoning will continue, and it may always be possible for the concept of human rights to become doubtful and subject to revision. But the best available public reasons so far seem to support its universal validity. Such public reasons include the arguments against genocide, slavery, and racial discrimination. Others have emerged from the kind of reasoning that reveals fallacies, confusions, and mistakes involved in the defence of Asian cultural exceptionalism.[8]

This contribution was published previously in *Report from the Institute for Philosophy and Public Policy*, University of Maryland, Vol. 16 (Spring 1996), No. 2, pp. 18-23.

NOTES

1. *The Straits Times*, Singapore (21 November 1992).
2. The Chinese government published the White Paper in response to criticism concerning human rights violations following its repression of the student demonstration on Tiananmen Square (Square of the Heavenly Peace) in 1989. Information Office, the State Council of the People's Republic of China, 'Human Rights in China', *Beijing Review*, Beijing, China, Vol. 34 (4-10 November 1991), No. 44.
3. *The Bangkok NGO Declaration on Human Rights* (27 March 1993), pp. 205-209.
4. *Ibid.*, note 3.
5. *Ibid.*
6. Information Office, the State Council of the People's Republic of China. 'The Progress of Human Rights in China', *China Daily*, Beijing, China (28 December 1995).
7. Amartya Sen. 'Our Culture, Their Culture', *The New Republic*, Washington (1 April 1996).
8. Other sources used: John Gray. 'After the New Liberalism', *Social Research*, New York, Vol. 61 (Fall 1994), No. 3, pp. 719-735; Yash Ghai. *Human Rights and Governance: The Asian Debate* (Occasional Paper Series No. 1), The Asian Foundation's Center for Asian Pacific Affairs, California, November 1994; Richard Rorty, 'Human Rights, Rationality, and Sentimentality', in Stephen Shule and Susan Hurley, Eds. (1993). *On Human Rights: The Oxford Amnesty Lectures 1993*. New York: Basic Books, pp. 111-134; Michael C. Davis, Ed. (1995). *Human Rights and Chinese Values: Legal, Philosophical, and Political Perspectives*. Hong Kong/New York: Oxford University Press.

F.A. Noor

Farish A. Noor is a Malaysian political scientist and human rights activist who is presently a research fellow with the working group 'Modernity and Islam' hosted by the Institute for Advanced Studies of Berlin. He has taught at the Centre for Civilisational Dialogue, University of Malaya, Kuala Lumpur, and worked as a journalist, contributing to a number of journals and newspapers in Malaysia and the United Kingdom. He is also the Secretary-General of the International Movement for a Just World (JUST), an international NGO based in Malaysia that campaigns for human rights while working with and within religious communities. He is currently researching the topic of political Islam in the Malay Archipelago and is writing a book on the Pan-Malaysian Islamic party, PAS.

3

BEYOND EUROCENTRISM

The Need for a Multicultural Understanding of Human Rights

Farish A. Noor

'I realized that if all the different races snore in the same language, then they must all be equal (before God).'
Malcolm X, after his pilgrimage to Mecca

We now live in a global environment where cultures and civilizations exist and interact closely with one another. In addition to furthering closer contacts, this new phenomenon for the peoples and nations of the world has also brought tension and conflict in the areas of culture, economics and politics. The different cultures of the world today are conscious of their cross-cultural similarities as well as the fundamental differences that have developed as a result of their different social histories and traditions.

In our rapidly changing global environment, we are now confronted with stark socio-political realities that cannot simply be ignored. Lifestyle and quality of life vary significantly among different sections of the globe. The lifestyles pursued in many of the developed areas of the world community have serious consequences for other areas of the world as well.

The different world-views and value systems have also elicited conflict in the area of human rights and fundamental liberties. Serious inequalities in human rights have come to light, and the hypocrisy or double standard of some global powers claiming to champion such values for the rest of humanity has become apparent.

This situation has resulted in several crucial issues that need to be addressed:

- Is there indeed a universal set of human rights?
- If so, how can such a concept or ideology of human rights be judged?
- Can different cultures, religions and traditions serve as guidelines for promoting human rights in their respective communities?
- What are the main obstacles to establishing such values?

Let me begin by stating quite unequivocally that in my view cultural differences are not a barrier to a global promotion of human rights and liberties. Concern to protect and promote fundamental human liberties and dignity exists in all cultures; it is part of the religious, philosophical, cultural and political discourses of the people themselves. The development of the concept of rights and liberties in traditional Malay culture illustrates this interest.

Determining the exact scope of the rubric of 'human rights' becomes necessary only when cultures at different levels of the global power structure impose their values on others. The issue also arises when particular political leaders use the concept of values (e.g. in the debate about Asian values) to suit their own political-strategic ends. The result in these cases is often a politics of cultural domination, a double standard or hypocrisy.

Overcoming these difficulties requires academic as well as practical approaches. Perhaps the most difficult is the way the ethnocentric perspectives of a number of powerful players have reduced the human rights debate in the world community to a monologue.

Eurocentrism and Essentialism

In the film *Ben Hur* (1959) the Roman centurion Marcellus tells his friend Juda Ben-Hur, 'There is only one reality in the world today. Look to the *West*, Juda!' Despite the fact that the Roman Empire collapsed under the weight of its own corruption and hypocrisy, the Western world continues to think of itself as the centre of not only the world but perhaps even the universe, much like the cultural imperialism of the past. Only a few years ago Francis Fukuyama, an American scholar, declared that the race to the 'end of history' was won by the West and that: 'The triumph of the West, of the Western idea, is evident first of all in the total exhaustion of viable systematic alternatives to Western liberalism.' We still live in the wake of past empires and caesars. To thinkers like Fukuyama, history has in fact come to an end in the static consumer culture of American shopping centres; there are no viable cultural, religious or traditional alternatives to the values and ideology of liberal capitalism.

The dominance of the Western world in politics and economics has mistakenly been interpreted by thinkers like Fukuyama, Huntington and others as a cultural and ideological ascendancy. The fact that the whole world is familiar with *Baywatch*, American fast food restaurants and Coca-Cola has been interpreted as an acceptance of Western lifestyle and values as well. So widespread is this misperception that many Western (particularly American) thinkers now believe that American values are indeed global ones and truly universal.

Such misperceptions can be designated as *ethnocentrism* or – more accurately – as *eurocentrism*. Ethnocentrism is the tendency of individuals and cultures to view themselves as well as the environment around them from the perspective of their own culture, values and beliefs. This point of view also entails a favourable evaluation of one's own culture while perceiving any differences from this norm as inferior, thus viewing relations between the self and the other as opposite extremes of a dialectic.

The term eurocentrism denotes the emerging perception within the European cultural, historical experience of European identity as good and all other forms as less good or less advanced. The cultural perspective from which the West views and judges the rest of the world by its own standards is much like the cultural superiority in vogue during the age of Empire.

The few Western thinkers who were sensitive to this problem have not addressed it very successfully. The recent writings of philosophers like Jacques Derrida and Jürgen Habermas betray the deep-rooted anxiety of Western (or, more precisely, Euro-American) thought in trying to come to terms with its own legacy of ethnocentrism/ eurocentrism and the problem of living in a multicultural world. Jacques Derrida, for example, questions where the socio-political and cultural development of the West (and Europe, in particular) will lead. In his book *The Other Heading (L'Autre Cap)*, he perceives Europe as torn between two alternatives: trying to retain its socio-political and cultural leadership (which Derrida admits is no longer possible) or coming to terms with its existence in a multi-centred world that has different cultural and political worldviews. If Europeans accept the validity of the different world-views, Derrida argues, besides maintaining their own Western value system, they will have to accept their inability to force such values on the rest of the world. They will need to accommodate the presence of alternative moral and ideological paradigms and negotiate the differences of culture and civilization in a radically altered world order. Derrida's main contention is that Europe can no longer force other cultures to accept its values and lifestyle because liberal democracy in the West has failed in many respects. Problems like racism, class divisions, economic oppression and socio-cultural inequalities have become too pervasive in the Western world. He submits that as long as the socio-economic and political problems and injustices within the West itself are not addressed, the Western world cannot serve as an example to the rest of the world.

Jürgen Habermas, a German philosopher, mentions a multicultural world order. He admits that Western democracy is not an ideology that can be taken out of its socio-historical context and simply exported to other parts of the world. He points to the ex-Soviet states of Eastern Europe as a notable example of the inability to transfer Western-style liberal democracy outside of its social and historical contexts.

There is another, parallel aspect to ethnocentrism/eurocentrism: the tendency of those who believe they are victims of ethnocentric prejudice to respond with a form of reverse ethnocentrism, to think in terms that can only be referred to as *essentialist*. Nowhere is this tendency to think in essentialist terms more apparent than in the debate on cultural values, especially 'Asian values'. While Western governments and elites have tried to impose their own ethnocentric/eurocentric values and beliefs on other communities and cultures, societies that feel threatened by

Western cultural domination are now beginning to adopt the idea of culturally-specific, exclusive values which are essential to their identity and need for protection.

We use the term *essentialism* to describe the tendency of individuals or cultural groups to base their sense of identity on rudimentary, fundamental 'essences', which can be understood in terms of cultural, historical, racial or even genetic particularities. This tendency has been used by many political groups to attain strategic goals. For example, the feminist writer Diana Fuss refers to this in her book *Essentially Speaking*. Political statements such as 'women are naturally more peace-loving than men' or 'women are naturally more caring than men,' used by feminists in the 1970s, were early examples of essentialist strategy.[1] But such assertions lack any serious intellectual support, for they are based on spurious notions of 'essential' differences in gender and genetics. The adoption of such strategies by a minority of Western feminist thinkers probably did more harm than good, for it further polarized gender differences between men and women and failed to provide feminism with a sound ideological basis for its long-term struggle.

Similarly, the use of the term 'Asian values' by some Asian elites and governments also rings hollow. Some Asian leaders even assert that Asians do not need human rights because human rights are not inherent in the 'Asian character' or an essentially Asian identity. Claims that Asians are naturally communal, naturally obedient to authority, or essentially conformist simply point to the intellectual bankruptcy of the elites and rulers who justify oppressing their own people in the most spurious, indefensible language.

This clash of perspectives has led to an impasse. The world is deadlocked in a struggle for hegemony, with the powerful, developed nations bent on imposing their cultural values as well as their political, economic and military dominance on the weaker ones. On the other hand, the economically weaker developing countries cling defensively to their cultural and religious traditions in a last-ditch attempt to salvage some sense of cultural autonomy and control over their identity. In doing so, the leaders of the weaker countries embrace a form of essentialist rhetoric, which is becoming increasingly reactionary, defensive and exclusivist. It becomes a vicious circle of ever-increasing antagonism, suspicion, and defensiveness, while the real issues of human rights abuses and the deterioration of human dignity remain unaddressed.

How can we break out of this vicious circle? First, concern for liberty and human dignity is common to all cultures and civilizations. Evidence from history and sociology shows that even the most 'primitive' societies have a deep-rooted understanding of issues related to power, rights and equity.

If the effort to secure, promote and defend the rights and freedoms of all peoples is to have a serious beginning, then we must accept that the world we are trying to save is a multicultural, multi-religious, and multiracial one. We will need to attempt to understand and appreciate the way different societies and cultures have developed their respective understandings of human dignity and values and to try to identify the specific local traditions and thought systems that should be elaborated to ensure that the goals are achieved.

To this end we need to learn to see through the eyes of the other and to see what the main concerns are from that viewpoint. The first step in negotiating the differences of culture and tradition is the search for authenticity, which goes deeper than a veneer of exclusive essentialism.

Tracing Authentic Sources: the Need for an Indigenous Understanding of Rights and Liberties

It is a gross error to say that the inspiration for democracy arises only from students and from foreign books. Any urge for democracy cannot be viewed only from above. We must look for it from below: from the position of the downtrodden, whose movements are under constant supervision and whose words are always muzzled.[2]

Western political leaders and observers who justify imposing their values on Asia by thinking of this region as a place where concerns for human rights and fundamental liberties are regarded as something new are clearly unaware of actual Asian culture, history and sensitivities. Moreover, they embody the type of essentialist (eurocentric) thinking mentioned above. Even a cursory examination of Asian history shows that concern for fundamental human rights has not only existed for centuries, but that it has been popularized in scholarly texts and religious scriptures, folk tales and popular humour. The theme, however, is usually voiced by those who are downtrodden, those 'whose movements are under constant supervision and whose words are always muzzled.'

During the twentieth century, several prominent activists and freedom fighters have emerged from all corners of Asia. Their political struggles have been predicated on the vocabulary and discourse of their culture and traditions. Mahatma Gandhi's struggle against British imperialism and the dominance of the developed world was based on the philosophical precepts of Hinduism; his approach, which embraced the essential unity and commonality of humankind, allowed him to transcend the boundaries of race and nationhood.

Today we see the rise of popular movements in many parts of Asia. The Philippines, Indonesia, Thailand and Myanmar[3] have experienced a renaissance of the values and beliefs of traditional philosophical and religious discourse, but now with concrete political goals such as emancipation and resistance. As Mikio Oishi explains, Aung San Suu Kyi's struggle against the repressive military junta that has held the people of Myanmar captive for more than three decades is a prime example of 'how an individual and a leader in Asia can harness the traditions and spiritual beliefs found in the country's culture and history and employ them to their fullest potential in the struggle against oppression and tyranny.'[4] Oishi also tries to correct many of the distortions that have come to be associated with Aung San Suu Kyi since her struggle first came to the attention of the world media. He notes that Suu Kyi is not a 'liberal' political activist according to this term's usual significance in the West. Her struggle against domination and tyranny also addresses the cultural and political domination of the Third World by the media and businesses of the developed capitalist West as well. Oishi argues that 'her conviction that human rights and democracy are important to Myanmar society' stems from her strong belief in the humanist principles of Buddhism and Burmese culture.[5] Oishi notes how these beliefs invariably colour the direction and tenor of her political struggle:

> In her numerous interviews and articles, she often refers to spiritual and moral values ... She discusses openly the concept of strength as a mental

and spiritual force. She is aware of the futility of any revolutionary move-
ment which does not possess spiritual and moral principles as part of its
goal. She praises Mahatma Gandhi's satyagraha (grasping the truth) and
ahimsa (non-violence). She extols the values of loving kindness, compas-
sion and equanimity over hatred, suspicion and coercion instead. [6]

In doing so Suu Kyi draws upon Myanmar's Buddhist-Burmese cultural traditions to establish a discursive foundation for a distinctly Myanmarese understanding of human rights and democracy. Furthermore, this gives her struggle an indigenous ideological basis for criticizing the current ruling military regime. From a traditional Buddhist perspective, the conduct of the military government, the State Law and Order Restoration Council (SLORC), has clearly fallen far short of the ideal of government described in the fundamental guidelines of Buddhism. The success of Suu Kyi's struggle among the people is thus understandable. As Oishi puts it:

By revealing the lawlessness and the anti-Buddhist nature of the SLORC
regime, and by presenting to the people an alternative social order which
is based on Myanmar's traditions and social values, Suu Kyi has become
a rallying point for the Myanmar people. It is also notable that, in her
confrontation with SLORC, Suu Kyi has achieved the moral high ground
firmly embedded in the Myanmar spiritual heritage. [7]

In this paper we will explore one type of discourse – *Islam* – to see how it has affected one part of Asia – *the Malay Archipelago*. We will show how this discourse has developed and will describe its potential as a discourse of political legitimation (as well as de-legitimation), and how it can be used as an ideological tool to secure fundamental rights and liberties for all. We will begin with a brief overview of the arrival of Islam to the Malay world and its massive socio-cultural impact.

Islam first arrived in Malaysia around the tenth and eleventh centuries, but the process of Islamization began much later, during the thirteenth and fourteenth centuries. The principal proselytisers were itinerant Muslim mystics and spiritual teachers (*Sufis*), whose own brand of spiritual Islam was both tolerant and accommodating toward the belief and value systems of the Indo-Malay peoples. Thus the Islamization of the Malay world was a peaceful, gradual process that began from the bottom: the lower strata of Malay society were converted first. The ruling elites were inclined to retain the traditional ideology of power and domination sanctioned by their own Malay-centric interpretation of Hindu-Buddhist *Dewaraja* (God-King) philosophy. Evidence of the elites' monopoly on Hindu-Buddhist discourse can be found in the remnants of these kingdoms themselves. Whatever classical literature, art and architecture still exists points to a particular, elite Indo-Malay interpretation of Hinduism and Buddhism aimed at deification and aggrandisement of the monarchs. The 'Hinduized' elite Malay culture that emerged over-emphasized epic, romantic interpretations of power and rule, while the subtleties of Hindu-Buddhist metaphysics and their traditions of critical thought and enquiry were neglected. Hinduized Malay court culture was raja-centric, court-oriented, exclusivist and distant from the society at large.

Works such as the Javanese court poet Prapancha's epic *Nagarakertagama* of the Majapahit kingdom glorified the ruler (King Hayam Wuruk) as the *Dewaraja*, placing him at the narrative centre of its Java-centric universe. It portrayed the ruler as a charismatic magnet, attracting wise Brahmins and untold riches 'to the land of Java (which was) becoming more and more famous for its blessed state throughout the world.'[8]

Yet the Hindu-Buddhist ideal of the benevolent and enlightened ruler guided by spiritual wisdom and an ascetic code of conduct was never truly realized by the rulers themselves. Even in the sphere of popular culture, the primary emphasis on the elite can be seen in the glorification of epic heroes such as Prince Rama (in the *Ramayana* epic) and the semi-divine Pandawa brothers (in the *Mahabharata*).

The differences in the socio-political environments of the Malay world before and after the coming of Islam are very significant. Before the dominance of Islam, the rulers incorporated elements and ideas from Hindu and Buddhist discourse that could be adapted to suit the needs of their traditional *adat*-oriented systems of rule and government.

The concept of *derhaka*, for instance, was taken from the discourse of Hinduism and Sanskrit and, after being imbued with sacred, supernatural connotations that gave it far greater authority, was re-contextualized into the Malay power structure. Barbara and Leonard Andaya have noted that *derhaka*, a word found repeatedly in Srivijayan inscriptions and meaning 'treason' to the ruler was adopted from Sanskrit to denote what became a heinous crime. The belief propagated by this Hinduized court culture was that treason and disloyalty to the king were tantamount to challenging the universal order itself and would bring calamity to the traitor as well as to the people in general.

Gradual consolidation of these new belief systems led to a court culture that grew increasingly restrictive and ritualistic. Andaya notes that this concept was so entrenched in Srivijayan statecraft that in the thirteenth century the Chinese customs official Chau Ju Kua believed that the personal followers of the Maharaja commonly killed themselves after their master died.[9]

The culmination of the elite monopoly and its 'engineering' of the discourses of Buddhism and Hinduism is the emergence of the concept of the Malay ruler as *Dewaraja*, a synthesis of Hindu and Buddhist concepts of leadership that took the form of a Shiva-Buddha cult, with the ruler at the apex of the realm and the pivotal point between earth and heaven. Moreover, it reinforced a tradition of authoritarianism where the maxim *quod principi placuit legis habit vigorem* was realized.[10]

It is thus hardly surprising that from the very beginning Islam appealed more to the Malay masses than to the rulers, for the universal appeal of Islam (as taught by the Sufis) was that the goal of self-perfection, the ideal *insanu'l-kamil*, could be attained by peasant and ruler alike, and in this quest all were equal. Furthermore, the Sufis taught that reason was universal, and that in this crucial respect all Muslims were equal as men and before God. As al-Attas says: within the Sufi interpretation of Islam, 'the essence of Man ... is that he is rational and rationality is the connection between him and reality. It is these concepts and that of the spiritual equality between man and man that gave the ordinary man a sense of worth and nobility denied to him in pre-Islamic times.'[11]

While the *kerajaan's* traditional court culture continued to exercise its monopoly over both symbolic and actual forms of power – concentrating them in the *Dewaraja* – Islam introduced a universal concept of a type of equality that ran counter to such total centralization. Islam's enormous appeal to the ordinary peasant is not surprising, and the conversions to Islam in the twelfth to fifteenth centuries became largely 'community affairs' (to use Taufik Abdullah's phrase), occurring outside the control, or possibly even the knowledge of the rulers themselves.[12] As A. Mukti Ali points out, Islam in the Indo-Malay world thus 'gave the small man a sense of individual worth as a member of an Islamic community,' while under the old regime, he would have been worth 'less than a grain of sand' beneath his ruler's immortal feet.[13]

The sense of individual worth appealed to the landless peasants, who were often pressed into forced labour or reduced to slavery to pay off their debts – a type of debt-bondage the ruling elite perpetuated. The elite of the Malay *kerajaan* (divine-monarchy) system became suspicious of the new creed and was concerned about the fact that it had caught on so quickly.

In the fifteenth century Islam had gained such an extensive following among the Indo-Malays that its ideology carried serious weight. By then the Malay kingdom of Melaka (Melacca) was established as the primary Malay-Muslim economic power within the region, and Islam was even making inroads in the ideological framework of the ruling elite. This process was halted only with the invasion of Melaka by the Portuguese in 1511, which led to the destruction of the kingdom and the collapse of its ruling house.

Before the Portuguese invasion, the Malay-Muslim power of Melaka had been a major trading centre of the Islamic and Asian worlds. Muslim traders from the *Hijaz*[14] and India considered it one of the most important port cities, and all trade routes in the East led to this capital of the Malay kingdom.[15] Nipur Chauduri writes that Melaka was one of the three main non-European metropoles of the international economic system in the pre-colonial era.[16]

Unfortunately, this made it a prize for the Europeans conquerors as well. Thus, a third party, European Christians, was added to the contenders in the region. The ideological struggle for hegemony between the Islamic reformers and the *kerajaan* – a struggle that had begun with the introduction of Islam in the fourteenth century and continued to the sixteenth century – was changed by the advent of this third contender. The third party was known as the *Ferenggi* (Franks), who were from Christian Europe. Their arrival in Southeast Asia, spurred by their conflict with their Islamic neighbours in the West, further complicated relations between the ruler and the Muslim masses.

In 1511, during the period when the *kerajaan* establishment of the Sultanate of Melaka was adapting to the creed of Islam ('domesticating' and ceremonially adapting it to its own needs), the Portuguese invaders arrived, led by Admiral Alfonso de Albuquerque. By then Melaka had become a well-known religious and political hub of Islamic teachings and Sufi activities. Al-Attas notes that 'by 1488, Melaka was already a centre for Sufism in the Malay archipelago' and that it attracted Muslim thinkers, scholars, sufis (and traders) from the entire Malay archipelago as well as the rest of Asia and the Muslim world.[17]

The *Risalat Hukum Kanun* (Melaka legal texts) notes that by that time substantial changes had been made to the Melakan *adat* laws by incorporating Islamic principles in such areas as marriage (*nikah*), family law, contracts, trusts (*wakaf*), loans, trade and belief.[18] And if the *Sejarah Melayu* is to be believed, the Sultan of Melaka himself was already making a humble effort to learn 'the sciences' of *Mu'amalat* (Islamic civil law) from the reclusive Maulana Yussof.[19] The influence of Islam on Melakan court culture might have been far greater had it not been for the catastrophe of 1511 when the Portuguese defeated the forces of Melaka and captured the city.

With the collapse of Melaka, the neighbouring Malay kingdoms of Aceh, Trengganu, Kelantan and Johor-Riau became the focal points of Malay-Muslim political and intellectual activity. In these kingdoms a new generation of critical Malay-Muslim scholars emerged whose work demonstrated the extent to which the Malay-Muslim world had become political. They articulated their concerns about rights, liberty, sovereignty and power publicly.

The work of the Malay-Muslim religious scholar Buchara al-Jauhari illustrates the development of Malay-Islamic thought and the extent of its popular appeal to the politicized masses. Nearly half a century before Thomas Hobbes' *Leviathan*,[20] Buchara al-Jauhari's *Taj-us Salatin, Mahkota Segala Raja-Raja* (The Crown of Kings, 1603) had already detailed the duties and responsibilities of the ruler towards his subjects, as well as the roles of the court and laws in defence of the people, restricting the power of the king. As Taufik Abdullah notes, the function of Islamic texts such as the *Taj-us Salatin* is clear: they define the parameters and guidelines for good government in Islamic terms, which inevitably reduces the ruler to the status of God's servant on earth. Furthermore, it places great emphasis on the role of the *pengawal raja*, the raja's advisors, ministers and *ulama* to ensure that the ruler does not deviate from the right path.

The first chapter of the *Taj-us Salatin* begins with a declaration of the universal equality of mankind as creatures and representatives of God on earth. Its Islamic ideology is embodied in the examples drawn from Islamic and Semitic history that illustrate the proper conduct of Muslim rulers. Citing the Prophet Muhammad as an exemplary ruler (Chapter 10), the *Taj-us Salatin* notes the necessary characteristics and obligations of the just Muslim ruler. These include the need:

- to ensure the prosperity and livelihood of his people;
- to protect his people from all manner of calamities (from poor government, abuse of power and invasions from abroad);
- to ensure the stability and prosperity of the country;
- to protect those who cannot protect themselves such as the poor, disabled, widows and orphans;
- to ensure that he chooses good advisors and listens to their counsel.[21]

Appreciating the importance of such texts for the Islamic world requires realizing the extent to which their moral and political vocabulary brought about a radical shift in the world-view of the *kerajaan*. What is radically different in the narrative of al-Jauhari's *Taj-us Salatin* (compared to most pre-Islamic *kerajaan* propaganda) is that it features a completely new organization of the world-view of the *kerajaan*. Whereas the traditional *kerajaan* view demands and expects loyalty from the *rakyat* (ordinary people) as the right of the ruler, the *Taj-us Salatin* demands the loyalty of all subjects to a supreme omniscient, omnipotent God, thus deflecting both loyalty and attention from the *rajas* themselves.

The emphasis on maintaining a ruler's just conduct is not empty rhetoric or religious homily: Al-Jauhari devotes several chapters to instructing courtiers, advisors and servants to the ruler. If the ruler requires guidance in seeking an advisor, al-Jauhari clearly spells out the

Islamic credentials a ruler ought to look for in his staff[22]:

> *And it is written in the* Qitab Sifat As-Salatin *that the ruler should always seek the company of those who are knowledgeable, and those who are engaged in matters of religion, and he should seek their instruction in all religious duties, and enquire about the characteristics of the pious, and remember what is taught to him.*[23]

These Islamic credentials are of crucial importance, because they ensure that the loyalty and obedience of the courtiers is to God, before the ruler or anyone else. The duties of these advisors include educating the king and instructing future monarchs, presenting all information that the ruler may require in detail and without hesitation, and reproaching the ruler if and when he transgresses the laws of Islam.[24] For the first time in the history of the *kerajaan's raja*-centric universe, the ruling ideology was opened to new participants and the site of political activity was extended beyond the person of the ruler to the courtiers, ministers, commanders, *qadhis*, *shiekhs* and advisors of the court:

> *And therefore it is necessary for the ruler who wishes to rule justly to have several advisors around him whose characteristics are their dedication, lack of greed and strength in their religious devotions; and they are to be sent to all corners of the realm so that they may see all that is good and bad about it, (and they) must relate the reports from his ministers and know of the deeds of his commanders as well as his servants, and know of the work of all his subjects; and all this must be conveyed without fail. Therefore the ruler must cultivate such a reliable staff around him.*[25]

All of these demands are articulated through an Islamic ethical discourse that focuses on the moral and political obligations toward God rather than the king alone. Rulers who violate the rules established by God will forfeit their right to rule,[26] resulting in a chaos and disorder that, by a strange coincidence, anticipates the Hobbesian account of the State of Nature described half a century later.[27]

Thus the thrust of al-Jauhari's critique is that no ruler is powerful enough to support the kingdom on his own: the survival and prosperity of the realm depend on the ruler ruling according to the dictates of his faith and abiding by its laws (which are, of course, the laws of God). Failure to do so leads to moral degradation, despair and, eventually, to total chaos and destruction. While symbolic power is left to the ruler, the true centre is shifted to that of a higher metaphysical level, beyond the reach of *rakyat* and *rajas* alike. For al-Jauhari this centre is clearly God and not the ruler. Only God is truly supreme, and it is God's will and commandments take precedence over those of the *raja*: 'And all the servants of the king must first of all place their fear in God Almighty above all else and before their king, and they must also hope for the bounty of God Almighty rather than their king.' [28]

In this philosophy the ruler is humbled, reduced to a symbolic instrument of God's will on Earth and an expression of this divine will. But even in this symbolic role, for al-Jauhari, the Muslim ruler is still required to possess and develop certain characteristics as prerequisites for the office of the *Khalifah al-Mu'minin*. Among these are faith, piety, charity, fairness and truthfulness. Quoting the *Kitab Fadhail al-Muluk*, al-Jauhari warns that the absence of any of these attributes immediately denies the ruler legitimacy as both a ruler and a Muslim:

> *Verily, Allah Ta'ala has demanded (that we be) fair and charitable. For from fairness comes truthfulness in all our deeds and all our words; and from charity comes kindness in all our labour and all our work and all our deeds; and these two virtues are found in all of mankind though in the ruler they are found most of all; and these two virtues, if they are not found in the ruler, then it cannot be said that the ruler is truly a ruler at all.* [29]

Bound thus by the code of Islamic law and the demands of faith and his role as the leader of the faithful, the *raja* has become an appendage to God (albeit within his own limited earthly kingdom). By placing the *raja* at the head of the state as the leader of the *Ummat*, al-Jauhari also entrusts him with the burden of maintaining the image of Islam. Simply put, the *raja* cannot be a good ruler without being a good practising Muslim. Although the *raja* is given no special privileges for his status as *raja*, al-Jauhari insists that he be carefully watched, as he is the living embodiment of the law he is charged to protect. So great is the responsibility of the ruler that al-Jauhari does not even afford him the luxury of food and sleep as he undertakes his task of government: 'And therefore the ruler should eat less and sleep less, and the ruler should never submit to his desires, so that he may be able to perform his duties of kingship which are such a great burdensome responsibility unto him.' [30]

But such mortal *rajas* could also fail in their tasks. The *Taj-us Salatin* seriously considers that a ruler may occasionally commit an indiscretion, and it describes appropriate remedies to deal with this, without allowing for divine intervention or even the revisions of court historians. The *Taj-us Salatin* informs the ruler who fails in his duties or does not care about his subjects that he has little chance of eternal salvation: 'And whichsoever king who fails to show pity to his subjects, Allah Ta'ala has forbidden him from entering heaven.'[31]

When a *raja* clearly does not act according to acceptable Islamic norms, al-Jauhari adds that he is no longer the ruler of his people, but their *enemy*.[32] Citing the story of Moses and his fight against the *Fir'aun* (Pharaoh) as an appropriate royal precedent, al-Jauhari permits rebellion against a godless tyrannical ruler, thus providing recourse for legitimate disobedience, revolt or even regicide, while remaining faithful to the tenets of Islam and the principles of Islamic law.

For Malay-Muslim scholars like al-Jauhari, Islam becomes a source of legitimation as well as de-legitimation. Thus the *Taj-us Salatin* and other Islamic texts were instrumental in building the foundations of a publicly accessible political discourse in which the social contract between *raja* and subject was radically reconfigured. Al-Jauhari's willingness to sanction rebellion and regicide as a final recourse from tyranny was unprecedented in the pre-Islamic era.

Buchara al-Jauhari's devastating polemic against unjust rule and tyranny is only one of many criticisms against all forms of oppression in the Malay world. In the centuries that followed, Islam provided the Malays with a philosophy for developing a political culture of resistance and empowerment when confronted by oppressive rulers from within as well as foreign enemies from without. In the seventeenth, eighteenth and nineteenth centuries, Islam was continually invoked to rally the Indo-Malay peoples against oppression from without. The struggle to liberate the Malay kingdoms of Patani, Perlis, Kedah, Kelantan and Trengganu from Siamese imperialism, for example, was waged in the name of Islam. So, too, was the struggle against British, Dutch, Spanish and later American imperialism.

In the following decades, Malay and Malay-Muslim thinkers such as Munshi Abdullah, Sayyid Shaykh al-Hadi, Hadji Agoes Salim, Sheikh

Abu Bakar al-Baqir, Kyai Haji Ahmad Dahlan, Tok Kenali and Hadji Omar Said Tjokroaminato were at the forefront of the resurgence of Islam and Islamic thought in the nineteenth and twentieth centuries. They were instrumental in the Islam's emergence as a discourse of modernization, social advancement and resistance to Western colonial rule. The writings of the radical Malay-Muslim thinker and political activist Dr. Burhanuddin al-Helmy, for instance, show how the Malay-Muslim intellectuals of the early twentieth century were concerned with questions of power, rights and sovereignty and address issues such as the politics of race, class and cultural imperialism.

The efforts of the radical Malay-Muslim activists were crucial in the struggle against British imperialism, just as the radical Malay-Muslim modernists were instrumental in the liberation of the Malays from the tyranny of their own elites. Malay women were among the first to benefit from their efforts, for it was the Malay progressive Muslims who led the movement for granting Muslim women equal rights to education, property ownership and participation in society as men.

But the path of progress is never straight, and the rise of Islam in the Malay world elicited major opposition. For example, British imperialism introduced a radical, unprecedented schism by separating religious power from state power. Under colonial rule Islam became a marginal force in the political arena at the same time that a decidedly eurocentric, secular political culture arose under the auspices of the colonial administrative and educational systems. During the closing stages of British colonial rule, the departing colonial power delivered another near-fatal blow to the development of Islam by collaborating with the ascendant Malay-aristocratic elite to destroy any revival of political Islam. The arrest of prominent Malay-Muslim thinkers and activists like Ustaz Abu Bakar al-Bakir and the destruction of the country's first Malay-Muslim political party (the *Hizbul Muslimin*) in 1948 complicated the survival of Islam in the post-colonial order.

To ensure that their own notion of liberal Islamic thought would dominate the public sphere, the emerging post-colonial elite tried to restrict critical Islamic discourse by using the state propaganda machinery and the tools of policing and national security for their own purposes. The Islamic opposition movement was also pulled in several contradictory directions, which resulted in the abandonment of many of its original progressive goals. (The Islamic opposition party, PAS, endorsed its own notion of ethnocentric, exclusivist pro-Malay communal politics in the 1970s, which was contrary to the universal political philosophy of its principal ideologist, Dr. Burhanuddin al-Helmy).

In Malaysia today there is little evidence of a dynamic, popular, local and traditional political philosophy among the people (unlike the situation in Myanmar, for example). The state's endorsement of its own 'liberal' and 'moderate' Islam has given rise to a popular religious discourse that is heavily monitored and controlled by the Home Office and the Ministry of Religious Affairs. The Ministry dictates what is orthodox. The resulting influence of traditional beliefs and the values of the feudal Malay *kerajaan* elite of the past on the predominant Malay-Islamic culture in the country today has become a serious obstacle to strengthening Malay political consciousness in the present era.[33]

Failure to form a pan-Malaysian political culture embracing the various strands of religious and cultural beliefs and values within this multiracial society has also precluded a pan-Malaysian popular local political philosophy to unite the people and give them a voice. In place of a popular pan-Malaysian discourse of rights and liberties, public discourse has adopted the commercial culture of Western consumerism, where the lowest common denominator has become the standard.

Obstacles

'This confusion is symbolic of our time: the leaders of the Third World appear to be confronting the oligarchy of the wealthy nations, but at the same time they are desperately envious of that position. Formerly, as colonial children, they were not even allowed into the ballpark with the colonial masters, and they rebelled. But did they rebel against the injustice, or did they rebel just so that they could get into the ballpark? Perhaps they can no longer tell. The revolution is over, before we really knew whom it was for.'

Goenawan Mohamad, *Cocktail Parties* [34]

Despite the fact that Asia retains a vast, seemingly endless repertoire of traditional belief and value systems, the traditional religious and cultural philosophies are being neglected in favour of a Western type of development. The extent to which current developments in Asia relate to Asian values and its religious and cultural traditions remains an open question.

The situation in present-day Malaysia embodies many of the complex and often contradictory elements in the socio-political climate. Certainly, the harsh treatment meted out to foreign migrant workers by the state has less in common with Malay-Islamic values than with those introduced during the colonial era. The state use of arbitrary executive powers is also more like the colonial period and pre-colonial feudal authoritarianism. The salient feature of most Asian nation-states today is their cavalier use of the tools of modernity (the state security apparatus, the police system and the machinery of propaganda). Equally important is their appeal to the theme of Asian values and traditional notions of respect towards authority.

These are among the factors that continue to stand in the way of a revival of traditional Asian discourses on rights and liberties. Two major obstacles to this revival are:

1) the tendency of the Asian elites to use the theme of Asian values strategically for political and economic ends;

2) the tendency of Western elites to assume that human rights can be guaranteed only if the Western model is exported everywhere.

Both these assumptions are fundamentally flawed. Concern for human rights, liberties and values are paramount in the developing world, and they need to be articulated appropriately in a public sphere. How can we achieve this?

Asians (as well as Europeans, Africans, Latin Americans and others) must solve the chronic socio-political problems in their own societies by turning to their own cultural resources. This entails reviving the progressive local cultural traditions and philosophies that have been long dormant.

For Malaysia this may mean revival of the critical, open, progressive tradition of Islamic thought that existed long ago. Islamic discourse and Muslim thinkers in Malaysia must revive the critical traditions that had once given Malay-Muslims the conceptual tools and guidelines for dealing with questions of power, equity, rights, liberties, race and gender relations.

The tradition of critical (as well as self-critical) Islamic thought in the Malay world and beyond appears in the work of many Muslim sources the world over. Recent examples in Malaysia include the emergence of groups like the Muslim women's movement *Sisters in Islam* (SIS). The importance of organizations such as these cannot be underestimated, for they ensure that Islamic discourse is not restricted to a small group of ideologues. By raising questions about how Islam can and should deal with the concerns of women, groups like SIS are constantly testing the limits of tolerance and acceptance.

Other developing societies need to tap into their own local traditions, religion, and culture. Recent events show that concerns for rights and liberties cannot be addressed simply by importing ideas and institutions from abroad. The attempt to 'democratize' Eastern Europe by injections of vast amounts of financial aid and establishment of democratic institutions such as judiciaries and parliaments failed, because these societies could not adapt to institutions and practices that had not evolved from their own socio-historical contexts. Nor will Asia and the rest of the non-Western world become democratic by blindly imitating the institutions and practices of the West.

If Asian societies are to secure their rights and liberties in a socio-political milieu that is culturally their own, they need to revive these cultural traditions by reviving the critical discourses contained therein as well. In the end this is the best way to ensure that their own governments and elite do not selectively manipulate the traditional values and beliefs as strategic tools of an essentialist discourse designed to deprive Asians of their rights in the name of Asian values.

As to the related problem of what the Western world should do, a few suggestions could be offered. The greatest obstacle to a universal understanding of human rights in the world today is the simple fact that the situation in this world is not one of equality. Despite the rhetoric about the so-called 'New World Order' and age of promise in the third millennium, we still live in a fragmented world that is torn apart by very real cleavages of power and interest. The gross inequalities and imbalances that favour the West (economically, politically, militarily and culturally) are the primary obstacles to protecting human rights worldwide – and this global inequality is itself a violation of human rights. NGOs, governments, organizations, corporations and individuals in the developed world will need to address this issue and be prepared to be self-critical in their analyses.

The hypocrisy of the West is the main reason why it has lost its moral and ideological leadership in the debate on human rights. Western governments that sell arms, chemical weapons and land mines to repressive regimes in other parts of the world have lost the moral high ground; they cannot lecture the rest of the world on issues of human rights and liberties. For example, the United States of America, which now promotes its image as the global defender and promoter of human rights, has been a superpower that has served as patron and benefactor to a number of repressive regimes the world over like Nicaragua, Chile, El Salvador, Saudi Arabia, Israel, Syria, Jordan, Pakistan, Indonesia (under Suharto) and the Philippines (under Marcos). Western society is in no position to preach to the rest of the world about environmental protection, consumption of resources, birth control and lifestyle when it is clear that the worst culprits – those who consume more, exploit more, pollute more and destroy more – live in the West. Non-governmental organizations and activists in the West would do better to combat the hypocrisy at their own doorstep before they attempt criticizing governments and societies in other parts of the world.

The superiority complex and parochial ethnocentrism that remains in the corridors of power in the West therefore needs to be dealt with in an honest, intelligent way. Many Western governments, non-governmental organizations and activists remain sceptical about the ability of different societies to establish a critical tradition of their own. The West's unstated but pervasive belief in its own cultural and ideological superiority remains the biggest obstacle to its coming to terms with genuine cultural differences on a global level. If we are to live in a truly equal and diversified multicultural global environment, the West will need to learn to respect difference and to understand other cultures. It will need to acknowledge and to try to comprehend the revival of the discourses of Islam, Hinduism and Buddhism in Asia as serious socio-political systems of thought and values. As Michel Foucault commented: 'The question of political Islam is a serious one which we (in the West) will have to face seriously. The first thing to do when facing this problem is not to confront it with fear or hatred.'

Conclusion

This essay has drawn on several examples from both historical and contemporary sources to show that concern for human rights is indeed a universal one, for all cultures and civilizations have raised the same questions in their local historical and socio-cultural contexts. These various cultural philosophies and traditions need to be revived to enable a fruitful exchange of ideas and viewpoints rather than the static monologue in which only those with power can speak – and others can only listen.

Living in a multicultural world, however, also means having to live with different, culturally-specific interpretations of fundamental values such as human rights and liberties. Just as different cultures have different ways of describing the object we refer to as water, different cultures have different myths, legends, stories and beliefs relating to the origin, use and value of water. This fact should not, however, lead us to think that what is water for one society is something entirely different in another. The object remains the same, although it may be viewed from a myriad of perspectives. There is no reason to believe that one of these perspectives is *essentially* better or more accurate than another.

The task that confronts all of us today, living in a globalized world that is contracting at an alarming rate, is to try to accommodate the many different perceptions and interpretations of the things we all value. While this may not be easy, the alternative is to reject the possibility of dialogue and to opt for the self-referential monologue of cultural authenticity or exclusivism instead. If we attempt to engage with the other, and if we try to appreciate the different cultural understandings of human rights and liberties, we will at least have taken the first step beyond the politics of essentialism and ethnocentrism.

By living in a world crowded with different cultural world views and value systems, we can experience the many possibilities that underlie the true meaning of pluralist universalism, which, though it is rooted in genuine differences, also embodies fundamental similarities. In our restless quest to negotiate our differences and respect each other, we may also learn, as Malcolm X did during his pilgrimage to Mecca, that while we speak different languages we all snore in the same one.

NOTES

1. Diana Fuss (1989). *Essentially Speaking: Feminism, Nature and Difference*. New York: Routledge.
2. Goenawan Mohamad (1994), 'Democracy', in *Sidelines: Writings from Tempo* (magazine banned in Indonesia 1994-8). Melbourne, Australia: Hyland House, p. 46.
3. The name Birma or Burma is still used, also by Aung San Suu Kyi and the democratic opposition. The current regime, State Law and Order Restoration Council (SLORC), introduced the name Myanmar.
4. Aung San Suu Kyi's struggle is described from a Buddhist perspective in the JUST Monograph: Mikio Oishi (1997). *Aung San Suu Kyi's Struggle: Its Principles and Strategy*. Penang, Malaysia: JUST World Trust.
5. *Ibid.*, p. 2.
6. *Ibid.*, pp. 5-6.
7. *Ibid.*, p. 11.
8. Theodore G. Pigeaud Th. (1960). *Java in the 14th Century: A Study in Cultural History*. The Hague: Martinus Nijhoff, p. 97.
9. Barbara Watson Andaya and Leonard Y. Andaya (1982). *A History of Malaysia*. London: MacMillan Press, p. 26.
10. Trans.: 'The whim of the prince has the force of law.'
11. Syed Naguib al-Attas (1993). *Some Aspects of Sufism as Understood and Practised Among the Malays*. Kuala Lumpur: Malaysian Sociological Research Institute (MSRI).
12. Taufik Abdullah (1993), 'The Formation of a Political Tradition in the Malay World', in Anthony Reid, Ed. *The Making of Islamic Discourse in Southeast Asia*. Monash University, Australia: Monash Papers on Southeast Asia No. 27, p. 39.
13. A. Mukti Ali (1970). *The Spread of Islam in Indonesia*. Yogyakarta, Indonesia: Jajasan NIDA, pp. 27-28.
14. The west coast of the Arabian peninsula was called the Hijaz, as opposed to the current Saudi Arabia.
15. See G.R. Tibbetts (1971). *Arab Navigation in the Indian Ocean before the Coming of the Portuguese: Being a translation of Kitab al-Fawa'id fi usul al-bahr wa'l-qawa'id of Ahmad ibn Majid al-Najdi*. London: Royal Asiatic Society of Great Britain and Ireland/Luzac Press.
16. K.N. Chaudhuri (1990). *Asia Before Europe: Economy and Civilization of the Indian Ocean from the Rise of Islam to 1750*. Cambridge and New York: Cambridge University Press.
17. Al-Attas, *op. cit.*, p. 51.

18. Azizan Abdul Razak (1980), 'The Law in Melaka Before and After the Coming of Islam', in *Tamadun Islam di Malaysia*. Kuala Lumpur: Persatuan Sejarah Malaysia (Malaysian History Society).

19. C.C. Brown (1952). *The Malay Annals, or Sejarah Melayu*. Oxford: Oxford University Press, pp. 124-125.

20. Thomas Hobbes' *Leviathan* was available only in 1651 in England. Hobbes began to work on the text while in exile in France in 1640-41. Al-Jauhari's *Taj-us Salatin* was composed and completed by 1603 in Aceh, North Sumatra.

21. Bukhair (Buchara) al-Jauhari (1603). *Taj-us Salatin*. Khalid Hussain (1966) Ed. Kuala Lumpur: Dewan Bahasa dan Pustaka.

22. The quotations from this book were translated by the author from Malay into English (editor's note).

23. Hussain, *op. cit.*, p. 75.

24. *Ibid.*, pp. 71-74.

25. *Ibid.*, p. 72.

26. 'Erti-nya hilang-lah daulat (raja) daripada sebab aniaya.' Translation: 'This means that he (the ruler) has lost his right to sovereignty due to his cruelty.' *Ibid.*, p. 73.

27. The account in the text reads: 'Therefore the people will despair, and cease to cultivate the land or to labour or to conduct their trade, all because of the misconduct of the ruler. And so the revenues of the King will lessen. And with the loss in revenue, so will the royal coffers be depleted. And when the coffers are empty, the *hulubalang* (guardian-chiefs) can no longer be maintained. And when the *hulubalang* are demoralized they will no longer carry out the ruler's commands. And when there is conflict and invasions, there will be no-one to defend the realm from such invasions, and so all will come to ruin and defeat, and the nobility and greatness of the ruler will be destroyed as well.' *Ibid.*, pp. 73-74.

28. *Ibid.*, p. 150.

29. *Ibid.*, p. 67.

30. *Ibid.*, p. 71.

31. *Ibid.*, p. 70.

32. A.C. Milner has noted the famous injunction in the *Taj-us Salatin*: 'Because the King is wrong, he has turned his face from Allah. Those who deviate from Allah's law and reject the Syariah are enemies of Allah and Allah's prophet. It is obligatory for us to treat the enemies of Allah as our enemies.' This, in effect, is probably one of the first attempts to give an Islamic licence to revolt against one's ruler in the *kerajaan* era, by turning a revolt into a holy war. See: A.C. Milner, 'Islam and Malay Kingship', in Ahmad Ibrahim, Sharon Siddique, Yasmin Hussain, Eds. (1985). *Readings on Islam in Southeast Asia*. Singapore: Institute of Southeast Asian Studies, p. 26.

33. The problems associated with the ongoing legacy of feudal thinking and values are discussed at length by Chandra Muzaffar in his work *Protector?*, which looks at the manner in which the traditional Malay feudal mentality and ideology have endured into the post-colonial era thanks to the political ascendancy of the aristocratic elites. As a result, the political culture of the Malay world right up

to the present has remained heavily influenced by feudal values, beliefs and practices, most of which are actually detrimental to and irreconcilable with the egalitarian ethos of Islam. See Chandra Muzaffar (1979). *Protector? An Analysis of the Concept and Practise of Loyalty in Leader-led Relationships within Malay Society.* Penang: Aliran Press.

34. Goenawan Mohamad, 'Cocktail Parties', in *Sidelines, op. cit.*, p. 83.

ANP/AFP/Roslan Rahman

Lee Kuan Yew was Prime Minister of Singapore from 1959 to 1990. Since then he has been Senior Minister.

Fareed Zakaria studied at Yale University and received a Ph.D. in Political Science from Harvard University (US). He is managing editor of *Foreign Affairs* and a contributing editor of *Newsweek*. He frequently writes in publications such as *The New York Times* and *The Wall Street Journal.*

4

CULTURE IS DESTINY

Fareed Zakaria in Conversation with Lee Kuan Yew

Meeting the Minister

'One of the asymmetries of history', wrote Henry Kissinger of Singapore's patriarch Lee Kuan Yew, 'is the lack of correspondence between the abilities of some leaders and the power of their countries'. Kissinger's one time boss, Richard Nixon, was even more flattering. He speculated that, had Lee lived in another time and another place, he might have 'attained the world stature of a Churchill, a Disraeli, or a Gladstone'.

This tag line of a big man on a small stage has been attached to Lee since the 1970s. Today, however, his stage does not look quite so small. Singapore's per capita GNP is now higher than that of its erstwhile colonizer, Great Britain. It has the world's busiest port, is the third-largest oil refiner and a major centre of global manufacturing and service industries. And this move from poverty to plenty has taken place within one generation. In 1965 Singapore ranked economically with Chile, Argentina and Mexico; today its per capita GNP is four or five times theirs.

Lee managed this miraculous transformation in Singapore's economy while maintaining tight political control over the country; Singapore's government can best be described as a 'soft' authoritarian regime, and at times it has not been so soft. He was Prime Minister of Singapore from its independence in 1959 (it became part of a federation with Malaysia in 1963 but was expelled in 1965) until 1990, when he allowed his deputy to succeed him. He is now 'Senior Minister' and still commands enormous influence and power in the country. Since his retirement, Lee has embarked on another career of sorts as a world-class pundit, speaking his mind with impolitic frankness. And what is often on his mind is American-style democracy and its perils. He travels often to East Asian capitals from Beijing to Hanoi to Manila dispensing advice on how to achieve economic growth while retaining political stability and control.

It is a formula that the governing elites of these countries are anxious to learn. The rulers of former British colonies have been spared the embarrassment of building grandiose monuments to house their offices; they simply occupy the ones that the British built. So it is with Singapore. The President, Prime Minister and Senior Minister work out of *Istana* (palace), the old colonial governor's house, a gleaming white bungalow surrounded by luxuriant lawns. The interior is modern – light wood panelling and leather sofas. The atmosphere is hushed. I waited in a large anteroom for the 'SM', which is how everybody refers to Lee. I did not wait long. The SM was standing in the middle of a large, sparsely furnished office. He is of medium build. His once-compact physique is now slightly shrunken. Still, he does not look seventy.

Lee Kuan Yew is unlike any politician I have met. There were no smiles, no jokes, no bonhomie. He looked straight at me – he has an inexpressive face but an intense gaze – shook hands and motioned toward one of the room's pale blue leather sofas (I had already been told by his press secretary on which one to sit). After thirty awkward seconds, I realized that there would be no small talk. I pressed the record button on my machine.

With the end of the Cold War, many Americans were surprised to hear growing criticism of their political and economic and social system from elites in East Asia, who were considered staunchly pro-American. What, in your view, is wrong with the American system?

It is not my business to tell people what's wrong with their system. It is my business to tell people not to foist their system indiscriminately on societies in which it will not work.

But you do not view the United States as a model for other countries?

As an East Asian looking at America, I find attractive and unattractive features. I like, for example, the free, easy and open relations between people regardless of social status, ethnicity or religion. And the things that I have always admired about America, as against the communist system, I still do: a certain openness in argument about what is good or bad for society; the accountability of public officials; none of the secrecy and terror that's part and parcel of communist government.

But as a total system, I find parts of it totally unacceptable: guns, drugs, violent crime, vagrancy, unbecoming behaviour in public – in sum the breakdown of civil society. The expansion of the right of the individual to behave or misbehave as he pleases has come at the expense of orderly society. In the East the main object is to have a well-ordered society so that everybody can have maximum enjoyment of his freedoms. This freedom can only exist in an ordered state and not in a natural state of contention and anarchy.

Let me give you an example that encapsulates the whole difference between America and Singapore. America has a vicious drug problem. How does it solve it? It goes around the world helping other anti-narcotic agencies to try and stop the suppliers. It pays for helicopters, defoliating agents and so on. And when it is provoked, it captures the president of Panama and brings him to trial in Florida. Singapore does not have that option. We can't go to Burma and capture warlords there. What we can do is to pass a law which says that any customs officer or policeman who sees anybody in Singapore behaving suspiciously, leading him to suspect the person is under the influence of drugs, can require that man to have his urine tested. If the sample is found to contain drugs, the man immediately goes for treatment. In America if you did that it would be an invasion of the individual's rights and you would be sued.

I was interested to read Colin Powell, when he was chairman of the Joint Chiefs of Staff, saying that the military followed our approach because when a recruit signs up he agrees that he can be tested. Now, I would have thought this kind of approach would be quite an effective way to deal with the terrible drug problem you have. But the idea of the inviolability of the individual has been turned into dogma. And yet nobody minds when the army goes and captures the president of another state and brings him to Florida and puts him in jail. I find that incomprehensible. And in any case this approach will not solve America's drug problem. Whereas with Singapore's way, we may not solve it, but we will lessen it considerably, as we have done.

Would it be fair to say that you admired America more 25 years ago? What, in your view, went wrong?

Yes, things have changed. I would hazard a guess that it has a lot to do with the erosion of the moral underpinnings of a society and the diminution of personal responsibility. The liberal, intellectual tradition that developed after World War II claimed that human beings had arrived at this perfect state where everybody would be better off if they were allowed to do their own thing and flourish. It has not worked out, and I doubt if it will. Certain basics about human nature do not change. Man needs a certain moral sense of right and wrong. There is such a thing called evil, and it is not the result of being a victim of society. You are just an evil man, prone to do evil things, and you have to be stopped from doing them. Westerners have abandoned an ethical basis for society, believing that all problems are solvable by a good government, which we in the East never believed possible.

Is such a fundamental shift in culture irreversible?

No, it is a swing of the pendulum. I think it will swing back. I don't know how long it will take, but there's already a backlash in America against failed social policies that have resulted in people urinating in public, in aggressive begging in the streets, in social breakdown.

The Asian Model

You say that your real concern is that this system not be foisted on other societies because it will not work there. Is there another viable model for political and economic development? Is there an 'Asian model'?

I don't think there is an Asian model as such. But Asian societies are unlike Western ones. The fundamental difference between Western concepts of society and government and East Asian concepts – when I say East Asians, I mean Korea, Japan, China, Vietnam, as distinct from Southeast Asia, which is a mix between the Sinic and the Indian, though Indian culture also emphasizes similar values – is that eastern societies believe that the individual exists in the context of his family. He is not pristine and separate. The family is part of the extended family, and then friends and the wider society. The ruler or the government does not try to provide for a person what the family best provides.

In the West, especially after World War II, the government came to be seen as so successful that it could fulfil all the obligations that in less modern societies are fulfilled by the family. This approach encouraged alternative families, single mothers for instance, believing that government could provide the support to make up for the absent father. This is a bold, Huxleyan view of life, but one from which I as an East Asian shy away. I would be afraid to experiment with it. I'm not sure what the consequences are, and I don't like the consequences that I see in the West. You will find this view widely shared in East Asia. It's not that we don't have single mothers here. We are also caught in the same social problems of change when we educate our women and they become independent financially and no longer need to put up with unhappy marriages. But there is grave disquiet when we break away from tested norms, and the tested norm is the family unit. It is the building brick of society.

There is a little Chinese aphorism which encapsulates this idea: *Xiushen qijia zhiguo pingtianxia. Xiushen* means look after yourself, cultivate yourself, do everything to make yourself useful; *Qijia*, look after the family; *Zhiguo*, look after your country; *Pingtianxia*, all is peaceful under heaven. We have a whole people immersed in these beliefs. My granddaughter has the name Xiu Qi. My son picked out the first two words, instructing his daughter to cultivate herself and look after her family. It is the basic concept of our civilization. Governments will come, governments will go, but this endures. We start with self-reliance. In the West today it is the opposite. The government says give me a popular mandate and I will solve all society's problems.

What would you do instead to address America's problems?

What would I do if I were an American? First, you must have order in society. Guns, drugs and violent crime all go together, threatening social order. Then the schools; when you have violence in schools, you are not going to have education, so you've got to put that right. Then you have to educate rigorously and train a whole generation of skilled, intelligent, knowledgeable people who can be productive. I would start off with basics, working on the individual, looking at him within the context of his family, his friends, his society. But the Westerner says I'll fix things at the top. One magic formula, one grand plan. I will wave a wand and everything will work out. It's an interesting theory but not a proven method.

Back to Basics

You are very sceptical of government's ability to solve deeper social issues. But you're more confident, certainly than many Americans are, in the government's ability to promote economic growth and technological advancement. Isn't this a contradiction?

No. We have focused on basics in Singapore. We used the family to push economic growth, factoring the ambitions of a person and his family into our planning. We have tried, for example, to improve the lot of children through education. The government can create a setting in which people can live happily and succeed and express themselves, but finally it is what people do with their lives that determines economic success or failure. Again, we were fortunate we had this cultural backdrop, the belief in thrift, hard work, filial piety and loyalty in the extended family, and, most of all, the respect for scholarship and learning.

There is, of course, another reason for our success. We have been able to create economic growth because we facilitated certain changes while we moved from an agricultural society to an industrial society. We had the advantage of knowing what the end result should be by looking at the West and later Japan. We knew where we were, and we knew where we had to go. We said to ourselves, 'Let's hasten, let's see if we can get there faster.' But soon we will face a different situation. In the near future, all of us will get to the stage of Japan. Where do we go next? How do we hasten getting there when we don't know where we're going? That will be a new situation.

Some people say that the Asian model is too rigid to adapt well to change. The sociologist Mancur Olson argues that national decline is caused most fundamentally by sclerosis – the rigidity of interest groups, firms, labour, capital and the state. An American-type system that is very flexible, laissez-faire and constantly adapting is better suited to the emerging era of rapid change than a government-directed economic policy and a Confucian value system.

That is an optimistic and attractive philosophy of life, and I hope it will come true. But if you look at societies over the millennia you find certain basic patterns. American civilization from the Pilgrim Fathers on is one of optimism and the growth of orderly government. History in China is one of dynasties which have risen and fallen, of the waxing and waning of societies. And through all that turbulence, the family, the extended family, the clan, has provided a kind of survival raft for the individual. Civilizations have collapsed, dynasties have been swept away by conquering hordes, but this life raft enables the civilization to carry on and get to its next phase.

Nobody here really believes that the government can provide in all circumstances. The government itself does not believe it. In the ultimate crisis, even in earthquakes and typhoons, it is your human relationships that will see you through. So the thesis you quote, that the government is always capable of reinventing itself in new shapes and forms, has not been proven in history. But the family and the way human relationships are structured, do increase the survival chances of its members. That has been tested over thousands of years in many different situations.

The Culture of Success

A key ingredient of national economic success in the past has been a culture of innovation and experimentation. During their rise to great wealth and power the centres of growth – Venice, Holland, Britain, the United States – all had an atmosphere of intellectual freedom in which new ideas, technologies, methods and products could emerge. In East Asian countries, however, the government frowns upon an open and free wheeling intellectual climate. Leaving aside any kind of human rights questions this raises, does it create a productivity problem?

Intellectually that sounds like a reasonable conclusion, but I'm not sure things will work out this way. The Japanese, for instance, have not been all that disadvantaged in creating new products. I think that if governments are aware of your thesis and of the need to test out new areas, to break out of existing formats, they can counter the trend. East Asians, who all share a tradition of strict discipline, respect for the teacher, no talking back to the teacher and rote learning, must make sure that there is this random intellectual search for new technologies and products. In any case, in a world where electronic communications are instantaneous, I do not see anyone lagging behind. Anything new that happens spreads quickly, whether it's superconductivity or some new life-style.

Would you agree with the World Bank report on East Asian economic success, which I interpret to have concluded that all the governments that succeeded got fundamentals right – encouraging savings and investment, keeping inflation low, providing high-quality education. The tinkering of industrial policies here and targeting sectors there was not as crucial an element in explaining these countries' extraordinary economic growth as were these basic factors.

I think the World Bank had a very difficult job. It had to write up these very, very complex series of situations. But there are cultural factors which have been lightly touched over, which deserved more weight. This would have made it a more complex study and of less universal application, but it would have been more accurate, explaining the differences, for example, between the Philippines and Taiwan.

If culture is so important, then countries with very different cultures may not, in fact, succeed in the way that East Asia did by getting economic fundamentals right. Are you not hopeful for the countries around the world that are liberalizing their economies?

Getting the fundamentals right would help, but these societies will not succeed in the same way as East Asia did because certain driving forces will be absent. If you have a culture that doesn't place much value in learning and scholarship and hard work and thrift and deferment of present enjoyment for future gain, the going will be much slower.

But, you know, the World Bank report's conclusions are part of the culture of America and, by extension, of international institutions. It had to present its findings in a bland and universalizable way, which I find unsatisfying because it doesn't grapple with the real problems. It makes the hopeful assumption that all men are equal, that people all over the world are the same. They are not. Groups of people develop different characteristics when they have evolved for thousands of years separately. Genetics and history interact. The Native American Indian is genetically of the same stock as the Mongoloids of East Asia – the Chinese, the Koreans and the Japanese. But one group got cut off after the Bering Straits melted away. Without that land bridge they were totally isolated in America for thousands of years. The other, in East Asia, met successive invading forces from Central Asia and interacted with waves of people moving back and forth. The two groups may share certain characteristics, for instance if you measure the shape of their skulls and so on, but if you start testing them you find that they are different, most particularly in their neurological development, and their cultural values. Now if you gloss over these kinds of issues because it is politically incorrect to study them, then you have laid a land mine for yourself. This is what leads to the disappointments with social policies, embarked upon in America with great enthusiasm and expectations, but which yield such meagre results. There isn't a willingness to see things in their stark reality. But then I am not being politically correct.

Culture may be important, but it does change. The Asian 'model' may prove to be a transitional phenomenon. After all, Western countries also went through a period in the eighteenth and nineteenth centuries when they were capitalist and had limited participatory democracy. Elites then worried – as you do today – that 'too much' democracy and 'too many' individual rights would destabilize social order. But as these societies modernized and as economic growth spread to all sections of society, things changed. Isn't East Asia changing because of a growing middle class that demands a say in its own future?

There is acute change in East Asia. We are agricultural societies that have industrialized within one or two generations. What happened in the West over 200 years or more is happening here in about fifty years or less. It is all crammed and crushed into a very tight time frame, so there are bound to be dislocations and malfunctions. If you look at the fast-growing countries – Korea, Thailand, Hong Kong, and Singapore – there's been one remarkable phenomenon: the rise of religion. Koreans have taken to Christianity in large numbers, I think some 25 per cent. This is a country that was never colonized by a Christian nation. The old customs and religions – ancestor worship, shamanism – no longer completely satisfy. There is a quest for some higher explanations about man's purpose, about why we are here. This is associated with periods of great stress in society. You will find in Japan that every time it goes through a period of stress new sects crop up and new religions proliferate. In Taiwan – and also in Hong Kong and Singapore – you see a rise in the number of new temples; Confucianist temples, Taoist temples and many Christian sects. We are all in the midst of very rapid change and at the same time we are all groping towards a destination which we hope will be identifiable with our past. We have left the past behind and there is an underlying unease that there will be nothing left of us which is part of the old. The Japanese have solved this problem to some extent. Japan has become an industrial society, while remaining essentially Japanese in its human relations. They have industrialized and shed some of their feudal values. The Taiwanese and the Koreans are trying to do the same. But whether these societies can preserve their core values and make this transition is a problem which they alone can solve. It is not something Americans can solve for them. Therefore, you will find people unreceptive to the idea that they be Westernized. Modernized, yes, in the sense that they have accepted the inevitability of science and technology and the change in the life-styles they bring.

But won't these economic and technological changes produce changes in the mind-sets of people?

It is not just mind-sets that would have to change but value systems. Let me give anecdotal evidence of this. Many Chinese families in Malaysia migrated in periods of stress, when there were race riots in Malaysia in the 1960s, and they settled in Australia and Canada. They did this for the sake of their children so that they would get a better education in the English language because then Malaysia was switching to Malay as its primary language. The children grew up, reached their late teens and left home. And suddenly the parents discovered the emptiness of the whole exercise. They had given their children a modern education in the English language and in the process lost their children altogether. That was a very sobering experience. Something less dramatic is happening in Singapore now because we are not bringing up our children in the same circumstances in which we grew up.

But these children are absorbing influences different from your generation. You say that knowledge, life-styles, culture all spread rapidly in this world. Will not the idea of democracy and individual rights also spread?

Let's not get into a debate on semantics. The system of government in China will change. It will change in Korea, Taiwan, Vietnam. It is changing in Singapore. But it will not end up like the American or British or French or German systems. What are we all seeking? A form of government that will be comfortable, because it meets our needs, is not oppressive, and maximizes our opportunities. And whether you have one-man, one-vote or some-men, one vote or other men, two votes, those are forms which should be worked out. I'm not intellectually convinced that one-man, one-vote is the best. We practise it because that's what the British bequeathed us and we haven't really found a need to challenge that. But I'm convinced, personally, that we would have a better system if we gave every man over the age of forty who has a family two votes because he's likely to be more careful, voting also for his children. He is more likely to vote in a serious way than a capricious young man under thirty. But we haven't found it necessary yet. If it became necessary we should do it. At the same time, once a person gets beyond 65, then it is a problem. Between the ages of forty and sixty is ideal, and at sixty they should go back to one vote, but that will be difficult to arrange.

Multicultural Schisms

Change is often most threatening when it occurs in multiethnic societies. You have been part of both a multiethnic state that failed and one that has succeeded. Malaysia was unwilling to allow what it saw as a Chinese city-state to be part of it and expelled Singapore from its federation in 1965. Singapore itself, however, exists peacefully as a multiethnic state. Is there a solution for those states that have ethnic and religious groups mixed within them?

Each state faces a different set of problems and I would be most reluctant to dish out general solutions. From my own experience, I would say, 'make haste slowly'. Nobody likes to lose his ethnic, cultural, religious, even linguistic identity. To exist as one state you need to share certain attributes, have things in common. If you pressure-cook you are in for problems. If you go gently, but steadily, the logic of events will bring about not assimilation, but integration. If I had tried to foist the English language on the people of Singapore I would have faced rebellion all around. If I had tried to foist the Chinese language, I'd have had immediate revolt and disaster. But I offered every parent a choice of English and their mother tongue, in whatever order they chose. By their free choice, plus the rewards of the marketplace over a period of thirty years, we have ended up with English first and the mother tongue second. We have switched one university already established in the Chinese language from Chinese into English. Had this change been forced in five or ten years instead of being done over thirty years – and by free choice – it would have been a disaster.

This sounds like a live-and-let-live kind of approach. Many Western countries, particularly the United States and France, respectively, have traditionally attempted to assimilate people toward a national mainstream – with English and French as the national language, respectively. Today this approach is being questioned, as you know, with some minority groups in the United States and France arguing for 'multiculturalism', which would allow distinct and unassimilated minority groups to coexist within the nation. How does this debate strike you as you read about it in Singapore?

You cannot have too many distinct components and be one nation. It makes interchangeability difficult. If you want complete separateness, then you should not come to live in the host country. But there are circumstances where it is wise to leave things be. For instance, all races in Singapore are eligible for jobs and for many other things. But we put the Muslims in a slightly different category because they are extremely sensitive about their customs, especially diet. In such matters one has to find a middle path between uniformity and a certain freedom to be somewhat different. I think it is wise to leave alone questions of fundamental beliefs and give time to sort matters out.

So you would look at the French handling of their Muslim minorities and say 'Go slow, don't push these people so hard.'

I would not want to say that because the French having ruled Algeria for many years know the kind of problems that they are faced with. My approach would be, if some Muslim girl insists on coming to school with her head-dress on and is prepared to put up with that discomfort, we should be prepared to put up with the strangeness. But if she joined the customs or immigration department where it would be confusing to the millions of people who stream through to have some customs officer looking different, she must wear the uniform. That approach has worked in Singapore so far.

Is Europe's Past Asia's Future?

Let me shift gears somewhat and ask you some questions about the international climate in East Asia. The part of the world you live in is experiencing the kind of growth that the West has experienced for the last 400 years. The West has not only been the world's great producer of wealth for four centuries, it has also been the world's great producer of war. Today East Asia is the locus of great and unsettling growth, with several newly rising powers close to each other, many with different political systems, historical animosities, border disputes, and all with ever-increasing quantities of arms. Should one look at this and ask whether Europe's past will be East Asia's future?

No, it's too simplistic. One reason why growth is likely to last for many years in East Asia – and this is just a guess – is that the peoples and the governments of East Asia have learned some powerful lessons about the viciousness and destructiveness of wars. Not only full-scale wars like in Korea, but guerrilla wars as in Vietnam, in Cambodia and in the jungles of Malaysia, Thailand, Indonesia and the Philippines. We all know that the more you engage in conflict, the poorer and the more desperate you become. Visit Cambodia and Vietnam; the world just passed them by. That lesson will live for a very long time, at least as long as this generation is alive.

The most unsettling change in an international system is the rise of a new great power. Can the rise of China be accommodated into the East Asian order? Isn't that kind of growth inevitably destabilizing?

I don't think we can speak in terms of just the East Asian order. The question is: can the world develop a system in which a country the size of China becomes part of the management of international peace and stability? Sometime in the next twenty or thirty years the world, by which I mean the major powers, will have to agree among themselves how to manage peace and stability, how to create a system that is both viable and fair. Wars between small countries won't destroy the whole world, but will only destroy themselves. But big conflicts between big powers will destroy the world many times over. That's just too disastrous to contemplate.

At the end of the last war what they could foresee was the United Nations. The hope was that the permanent five would maintain the rule of law or gradually spread the rule of law in international relations. It did not come off because of Stalin and the Cold War. This is now a new phase. The great powers – by which I mean America, Western Europe as a group if they become a union, Japan, China and, in twenty to thirty years time, the Russian republic – have got to find a balance between themselves. I think the best way forward is through the United Nations. It already has 48 years of experience. It is imperfect, but what is the alternative? You can not have a consortium of five big powers lording it over the rest of mankind. They will not have the moral authority or legitimacy to do it. Are they going to divide the world into five spheres of influence? So they have to fall back on some multilateral framework and work out a set of rules that makes it viable. There may be conflicts of a minor nature, for instance between two Latin American countries or two small Southeast Asian countries; that doesn't really matter. Now if you have two big countries in South Asia like India and Pakistan and both with nuclear capabilities, then something has to be done. It is in that context that we have to find a place for China when it becomes a major economic and military power.

Is the Chinese regime stable? Is the growth that's going on there sustainable? Is the balancing act between economic reform and political control that Deng Xiaoping is trying to keep going sustainable after his death?

The regime in Beijing is more stable than any alternative government that can be formed in China. Let us assume that the students had carried the day at Tiananmen and they had formed a government. The same students who were at Tiananmen went to France and America. They've been quarrelling with each other ever since. What kind of China would they have today? Something worse than the Soviet Union. China is a vast, disparate country; there is no alternative to strong central power.

Do you worry that the kind of rapid and unequal growth taking place in China might cause the country to break up?

First, the economy is growing everywhere, even in Sichuan, in the heart of the interior. Disparate growth rates are inevitable. It is the difference between, say, California before the recession and the Rust Belt. There will be enormous stresses because of the size of the country and the intractable nature of the problems – the poor infrastructure, the weak institutions, the wrong systems that they have installed, modelling themselves upon the Soviet system in Stalin's time. Given all those handicaps, I am amazed that they have got so far.

What about the other great East Asian power? If Japan continues on the current trajectory, should the world encourage the expansion of its political and military responsibilities and power?

No. I know that the present generation of Japanese leaders do not want to project power. I'm not sure what follows when leaders born after the war take charge. I doubt if there will be a sudden change. If Japan can carry on with its current policy, leaving security to the Americans and concentrating on the economic and the political, the world will be better off. And the Japanese are quite happy to do this. It is when America feels that it's too burdensome and not worth the candle to be present in East Asia to protect Japan that it will have to look after its own security. When Japan becomes a separate player, it is an extra joker in the pack of cards.

You've said recently that allowing Japan to send its forces abroad is like giving liquor to an alcoholic.

The Japanese have always had this cultural trait, that whatever they do they carry it to the nth degree. I think they know this. I have Japanese friends who have told me this. They admit that this is a problem with them.

What if Japan did follow the trajectory that most great powers have; that it was not content simply to be an economic superpower, 'a bank with a flag' in a writer's phrase? What if they decided they wanted to have the ultimate mark of a great power – nuclear weapons? What should the world do?

If they decided on that the world will not be able to stop them. You are unable to stop North Korea. Nobody believes that an American government that could not sustain its mission in Somalia because of an ambush and one television snippet of a dead American pulled through the streets in Mogadishu could contemplate a strike on North Korean nuclear facilities like the Israeli strike on Iraq. Therefore it can only be sanctions in the UN Security Council. That requires that there be no vetoes. Similarly, if the Japanese decide to go nuclear, I don't believe you will be able to stop them. But they know that they face a nuclear power in China and in Russia, and so they would have to posture themselves in such a way as not to invite a pre-emptive strike. If they can avoid a pre-emptive strike then a balance will be established. Each will deter the others.

So it's the transition period that you are worried about.

I would prefer that the matter never arises and I believe so does the world. Whether the Japanese go down the military path will depend largely on America's strength and its willingness to be engaged.

Vive la Différence

Is there some contradiction here between your role as a politician and your new role as an intellectual, speaking out on all matters? As a politician you want America as a strong balancer in the region, a country that is feared and respected all over the world. As an intellectual, however, you choose to speak out forcefully against the American model in a way that has to undermine America's credibility abroad.

That's preposterous. The last thing I would want to do is to undermine her credibility. America has been unusual in the history of the world, being the sole possessor of power – the nuclear weapon – and the one and only government in the world unaffected by war damage whilst the others were in ruins. Any old and established nation would have ensured its supremacy for as long as it could. But America set out to put her defeated enemies on their feet, to ward off an evil force, the Soviet Union, brought about technological change by transferring technology generously and freely to Europeans and to Japanese, and enabled them to become her challengers within thirty years. By 1975 they were at her heels. That's unprecedented in history. There was a certain greatness of spirit born out of the fear of communism plus American idealism that brought that about. But that does not mean that we all admire everything about America.

Let me be frank; if we did not have the good points of the West to guide us, we wouldn't have got out of our backwardness. We would have been a backward economy with a backward society. But we do not want all of the West.

A Coda on Culture

The dominant theme throughout our conversation was culture. Lee returned again and again to his views on the importance of culture and the differences between Confucianism and Western values. In this respect, Lee is very much part of a trend. Culture is in. From business consultants to military strategists, people talk about culture as the deepest and most determinative aspect of human life.

I remain sceptical. If culture is destiny, what explains a culture's failure in one era and success in another? If Confucianism explains the economic boom in East Asia today, does it not also explain that region's stagnation for four centuries? In fact, when East Asia seemed immutably poor, many scholars – most famously Max Weber – made precisely that case, arguing that Confucian-based cultures discouraged all the attributes necessary for success in capitalism. Today scholars explain how Confucianism emphasizes the essential traits for economic dynamism. Were Latin American countries to succeed in the next few decades, we shall surely read encomiums to Latin culture. I suspect that since we cannot find one simple answer to why certain societies succeed at certain times, we examine successful societies and search within their cultures for the seeds of success. Cultures being complex, one finds in them what one wants.

What explains Lee Kuan Yew's fascination with culture? It is not something he was born with. Until his thirties he was called 'Harry' Lee (and still is by family and friends). In the 1960s the British foreign secretary could say to him, 'Harry, you're the best bloody Englishman east of the Suez.' This is not a man untouched by the West. Part of his interest in cultural differences is surely that they provide a coherent defence against what he sees as Western democratic imperialism. But a deeper reason is revealed in something he said in our conversation: 'We have left the past behind, and there is an underlying unease that there will be nothing left of us which is part of the old.'

Cultures change. Under the impact of economic growth, technological change and social transformation, no culture has remained the same. Most of the attributes that Lee sees in eastern cultures were once part of the West. Four hundred years of economic growth changed things. From the very beginning of England's economic boom, many Englishmen worried that as their country became rich it was losing its moral and ethical base. 'Wealth accumulates and men decay,' wrote Oliver Goldsmith in 1770. It is this 'decay' that Lee is trying to stave off. He speaks of the anxious search for religion in East Asia today, and while he never says this, his own quest for a Confucian alternative to the West is part of this search. But to be modern without becoming more Western is difficult; the two are not wholly separable. The West has left a mark on 'the rest', and it is not simply a legacy of technology and material products. It is, perhaps most profoundly, in the realm of ideas.

At the close of the interview Lee handed me three pages. This was, he explained, to emphasize how alien Confucian culture is to the West. The pages were from the book *East Asia: Tradition and Transformation*, by John Fairbank,[1] an American scholar.

This contribution was published previously in *Foreign Affairs*, Vol. 73 (March/April 1994), No. 2, pp. 109-126.

NOTES

1. John King Fairbank *et al.* (1976). *East Asia: Tradition and Transformation.* Boston: Houghton Mifflin (published previously by Allen and Unwin, London, 1973).

National Congress for New Politics, South Korea

Kim Dae Jung has been a human rights activist for more than forty years, a political prisoner and a dissident. He was Chairman of the Kim Dae Jung Peace Foundation for the Asia-Pacific Region until 1997. Since early 1998 he has been President of the Republic of Korea (South Korea).

5

IS CULTURE DESTINY?

The Myth of Asia's Anti-Democratic Values
A Response to Lee Kuan Yew

Kim Dae Jung

In his interview with *Foreign Affairs* (March/April 1994), Singapore's former Prime Minister, Lee Kuan Yew, presents interesting ideas about cultural differences between Western and East Asian societies and the political implications of those differences. Although he does not explicitly say so, his statements throughout the interview and his track record make it obvious that his admonition to Americans 'not to foist their system indiscriminately on societies in which it will not work' implies that Western-style democracy is not applicable to East Asia. Considering the esteem in which he is held among world leaders and the prestige of this journal, this kind of argument is likely to have considerable impact and therefore deserves a careful reply.

With the collapse of the Soviet Union in 1991, socialism has been in retreat. Some people conclude that the Soviet demise was the result of the victory of capitalism over socialism. But I believe it represented the triumph of democracy over dictatorship. Without democracy, capitalism in Prussian Germany and Meiji Japan eventually met its tragic end. The many Latin American states that in recent decades embraced capitalism while rejecting democracy failed miserably. On the other hand, countries practising democratic capitalism or democratic socialism, despite temporary setbacks, have prospered.

In spite of these trends, lingering doubts remain about the applicability of and prospects for democracy in Asia. Such doubts have been raised mainly by Asia's authoritarian leaders, Lee being the most articulate among them. They have long maintained that cultural differences make the 'Western concept' of democracy and human rights inapplicable to East Asia. Does Asia have the philosophical and historical underpinnings suitable for democracy? Is democracy achievable there?

Self-serving Self-reliance

Lee stresses cultural factors throughout his interview. I too believe in the importance of culture, but I do not think it alone determines a society's fate, nor is it immutable. Moreover, Lee's view of Asian cultures is not only unsupportable but self-serving. He argues that eastern societies, unlike Western ones, 'believe that the individual exists in the context of his family' and that the family is 'the building brick of society'. However, as an inevitable consequence of industrialization, the family-centred East Asian societies are also rapidly moving toward self-centred individualism. Nothing in human history is permanent.

Lee asserts that, in the East, 'the ruler or the government does not try to provide for a person what the family best provides.' He cites this ostensibly self-reliant, family-oriented culture as the main cause of East Asia's economic successes and ridicules Western governments for allegedly trying to solve all of society's problems, even as he worries about the moral breakdown of Western societies due to too much democracy and too many individual rights. Consequently, according to Lee, the Western political system, with its intrusive government, is not suited to family-oriented East Asia. He rejects Westernization while embracing modernization and its attendant changes in lifestyle – again strongly implying that democracy will not work in Asia.

Family Values (required here)

But the facts demonstrate just the opposite. It is not true, as Lee alleges, that Asian governments shy away from intervening in private matters and taking on all of society's problems. Asian governments intrude much more than Western governments into the daily affairs of individuals and families. In Korea, for example, each household is required to attend monthly neighbourhood meetings to receive government directives and discuss local affairs. Japan's powerful government constantly intrudes into the business world to protect perceived national interests, to the point of causing disputes with the United States and other trading partners. In Lee's Singapore, the government stringently regulates individuals' actions – such as chewing bubble-gum, spitting, smoking, littering, and so on – to an Orwellian extreme of social engineering. Such facts fly in the face of his assertion that East Asia's governments are minimalist. Lee makes these false claims to justify his rejection of Western-style democracy. He even dislikes the one man, one vote principle, so fundamental to modern democracy, saying that he is not 'intellectually convinced' it is best.

Opinions like Lee's hold considerable sway not only in Asia but among some Westerners because of the moral breakdown of many advanced democratic societies. Many Americans thought, for example, that the US citizen Michael Fay deserved the caning he received from Singaporean authorities for his act of vandalism. However, moral breakdown is attributable not to inherent shortcomings of Western cultures, but to those of industrial societies; a similar phenomenon is now spreading through Asia's newly industrializing societies. The fact that Lee's Singapore, a small city-state, needs a near-totalitarian police state to assert control over its citizens contradicts his assertion that everything would be all right if governments would refrain from interfering in the private affairs of the family. The proper way to cure the ills of industrial societies is not to impose the terror of a police state but to emphasize ethical education, give high regard to spiritual values, and promote high standards in culture and the arts.

Long Before Locke

No one can argue with Lee's objection to 'foisting' an alien system 'indiscriminately on societies in which it will not work'. The question is whether democracy is a system so alien to Asian cultures that it will not work. Moreover, considering Lee's record of absolute intolerance of dissent and the continued crackdown on dissidents in many other Asian countries, one is also compelled to ask whether democracy has been given a chance in places like Singapore.

A thorough analysis makes it clear that Asia has a rich heritage of democracy-oriented philosophies and traditions. Asia has already made great strides toward democratization and possesses the necessary conditions to develop democracy even beyond the level of the West.

Democratic Ideals

It is widely accepted that the English political philosopher John Locke laid the foundation for modern democracy. According to Locke, sovereign rights reside with the people and, based on a contract with the people, leaders are given a mandate to govern, which the people can withdraw. But almost two millennia before Locke, Chinese philosopher Meng Tzu preached similar ideas. According to his 'Politics of Royal Ways', the king is the 'Son of Heaven', and heaven bestowed on its son a mandate to provide good government, that is, to provide good for the people. If he did not govern righteously, the people had the right to rise up and overthrow his government in the name of heaven. Meng Tzu even justified regicide, saying that once a king loses the mandate of heaven he is no longer worthy of his subjects' loyalty. The people came first, Meng Tzu said, the country second, and the king third. The ancient Chinese philosophy of *Minben Zhengchi*, or 'people-based politics', teaches that 'the will of the people is the will of heaven' and that one should 'respect the people as heaven' itself.

A native religion of Korea, Tonghak, went even further, advocating that 'man is heaven' and that one must serve man as one does heaven. These ideas inspired and motivated nearly half a million peasants in 1894 to revolt against exploitation by feudalistic government internally and imperialistic forces externally. There are no ideas more fundamental to democracy than the teachings of Confucianism, Buddhism, and Tonghak. Clearly, Asia has democratic philosophies as profound as those of the West.

Democratic Institutions

Asia also has many democratic traditions. When Western societies were still being ruled by a succession of feudal lords, China and Korea had already sustained county prefecture systems for about 2,000 years. The government of the Chin Dynasty, founded by Chin Shih Huang Ti (literally, the founder of Chin), practised the rule of law and saw to it that everyone, regardless of class, was treated fairly. For nearly 1,000 years in China and Korea, even the sons of high-ranking officials were not appointed to important official positions unless they passed civil service examinations. These stringent tests were administered to members of the aristocratic class, who constituted over ten per cent of the population, thus guaranteeing equal opportunity and social mobility, which are so central to popular democracy. This practice sharply contrasted with that of European fiefdoms of that time, where pedigree more or less determined one's official position. In China and Korea powerful boards of censors acted as a check against imperial misrule and abuses by government officials. Freedom of speech was highly valued, based on the understanding that the nation's fate depended on it. Confucian scholars were taught that remonstration against an erring monarch was a paramount duty. Many civil servants and promising political elites gave their lives to protect the right to free speech.

The fundamental ideas and traditions necessary for democracy existed in both Europe and Asia. Although Asians developed these ideas long before the Europeans did, Europeans formalized comprehensive and effective electoral democracy first. The invention of the electoral system is Europe's greatest accomplishment. The fact that this system was developed elsewhere does not mean that 'it will not work' in Asia. Many Asian countries, including Singapore, have become prosperous after adopting a 'Western' free-market economy, which is such an integral part of a democracy. Incidentally, in countries where economic development preceded political advancement – Germany, Italy, Japan, Spain – it was only a matter of time before democracy followed.

The State of Democracy in Asia

The best proof that democracy can work in Asia is the fact that, despite the stubborn resistance of authoritarian rulers like Lee, Asia has made great strides toward democracy. In fact, Asia has achieved the most remarkable record of democratization of any region since

1974. By 1990 a majority of Asian countries were democracies, compared to a 45 per cent democratization rate worldwide.[1] This achievement has been overshadowed by Asia's tremendous economic success. I believe democracy will take root throughout Asia around the start of the twenty-first century. By the end of its first quarter, Asia will witness an era not only of economic prosperity, but also of flourishing democracy.

I am optimistic for several reasons. The Asian economies are moving from a capital- and labour-intensive industrial phase into an information- and technology-intensive one. Many experts have acknowledged that this new economic world order requires guaranteed freedom of information and creativity. These things are possible only in a democratic society. Thus Asia has no practical alternative to democracy; it is a matter of survival in an age of intensifying global economic competition. The world economy's changes have already meant a greater and easier flow of information, which has helped Asia's democratization process.

Democracy has been consistently practised in Japan and India since the end of World War II. In Korea, Burma, Taiwan, Thailand, Pakistan, the Philippines, Bangladesh, Sri Lanka, and other countries, democracy has been frustrated at times, even suspended. Nevertheless, most of these countries have democratized, and in all of them, a resilient 'people power' has been demonstrated through elections and popular movements. Even in Thailand, after ten military governments, a civilian government has finally emerged. The Mongolian government, after a long period of one-party dictatorship, has also voluntarily accepted democracy. The fundamental reason for my optimism is this increasing awareness of the importance of democracy and human rights among Asians themselves and their willingness to make the necessary efforts to realize these goals. Despite many tribulations, the torch of democracy continues to burn in Asia because of the aspirations of its people.

We are the World

As Asians increasingly embrace democratic values, they have the opportunity and obligation to learn from older democracies. The West has experienced many problems in realizing its democratic systems. It is instructive, for example, to remember that Europeans practised democracy within the boundaries of their nation-states but not outside. Until recently, the Western democracies coddled the interests of a small propertied class. The democracies that benefited much broader majorities through socio-economic investments were mostly established after World War II. Today, we must start with a rebirth of democracy that promotes freedom, prosperity, and justice both within each country and among nations, including the less-developed countries: a global democracy.

Instead of making Western culture the scapegoat for the disruptions of rapid economic change, it is more appropriate to look at how the traditional strengths of Asian society can provide for a better democracy. In Asia, democracy can encourage greater self-reliance while respecting cultural values. Such a democracy is the only true expression of a people, but it requires the full participation of all elements of society. Only then will it have legitimacy and reflect a country's vision.

Asian authoritarians misunderstand the relationship between the rules of effective governance and the concept of legitimacy. Policies that try to protect people from the bad elements of economic and social change will never be effective if imposed without consent; the same policies, arrived at through public debate, will have the strength of Asia's proud and self-reliant people.

A global democracy will recognize the connection between how we treat each other and how we treat nature, and it will pursue policies that benefit future generations. Today we are threatening the survival of our environment through wholesale destruction and endangerment of all species. Our democracy must become global in the sense that it extends to the skies, the earth, and all things with brotherly affection.

The Confucian maxim *Xiushen qijia zhiguo pingtianxia*, which offers counsel toward the ideal of 'great peace under heaven', shows an appreciation for judicious government. The ultimate goal in Confucian political philosophy, as stated in this aphorism, is to bring peace under heaven (*pingtianxia*). To do so, one must first be able to keep one's own household in order (*qijia*), which in turn requires that one cultivate 'self' (*xiushen*). This teaching is a political philosophy that emphasizes the role of government and stresses the ruling elite's moral obligation to strive to bring about peace under heaven. Public safety, national security, and water and forest management are deemed critical. This concept of peace under heaven should be interpreted to include peaceful living and existence for all things under heaven. Such an understanding can also be derived from Gautama Buddha's teaching that all creatures and things possess a Buddha-like quality.

Since the fifth century BC, the world has witnessed a series of revolutions in thought. Chinese, Indian, Greek, and Jewish thinkers have led great revolutions in ideas, and we are still living under the influence of their insights. However, for the past several hundred years, the world has been dominated by Greek and Judeo-Christian ideas and traditions. Now it is time for the world to turn to China, India, and the rest of Asia for another revolution in ideas. We need to strive for a new democracy that guarantees the right of personal development for all human beings and the wholesome existence of all living things.

A natural first step toward realizing such a new democracy would be full adherence to the Universal Declaration of Human Rights, adopted by the United Nations in 1948. This international document reflects basic respect for the dignity of people, and Asian nations should take the lead in implementing it.

The movement for democracy in Asia has been carried forward mainly by Asia's small but effective army of dedicated people in and out of political parties, encouraged by non-governmental and quasi-governmental organizations for democratic development from around the world. These are hopeful signs for Asia's democratic future. Such groups are gaining in their ability to force governments to listen to the concerns of their people, and they should be supported.

Asia should lose no time in firmly establishing democracy and strengthening human rights. The biggest obstacle is not its cultural heritage but the resistance of authoritarian rulers and their apologists. Asia has much to offer the rest of the world; its rich heritage of democracy-oriented philosophies and traditions can make a significant contribution to the evolution of global democracy. Culture is not necessarily our destiny. Democracy is.

This contribution was published previously in *Foreign Affairs*, Vol. 73 (November/December 1994), No. 6, pp. 189-194.

NOTES

1. Samuel P. Huntington (1991). *The Third Wave: Democratization in the Late Twentieth Century.* Norman: University of Oklahoma Press.

KUB/VEB Tilburg

Willem van Genugten is Professor of International Law at Tilburg University and Professor of Human Rights at Nijmegen University. He also serves on the Human Rights Commission of the Advisory Council for International Affairs to the Dutch government.

6

HUMAN RIGHTS ARE NOT FOR SALE

On Universality and Conditionality

Willem van Genugten

Should trade relations be used to achieve human rights? This question is the focus of the present contribution, which deals with the World Trade Organization (WTO) and the European Community/European Union (EC/EU).[1] First, however, I will consider whether human rights are universal and will examine the margin of appreciation that states should have in implementing them. After all, these aspects need to be clarified to offer a balanced view of the role human rights should play in international economic relations.

Universality and the 'Margin of Appreciation'

All over the world, people are entitled to live in dignity, although what such an existence entails will always be a subject of debate. I find the Universal Declaration of Human Rights (1948) a convenient reference. On living in dignity, this declaration mentions equality before the law (Article 7), not being subject to arbitrary arrest (Article 9), the right to nationality (Article 15) and freedom of conscience and religion (Article 18). The declaration further states that the individual should be entitled to:

the right to a standard of living adequate for the health and well-being of himself and of his family, including food, clothing, housing and medical care and necessary social services, and the right to a provision in the event of unemployment, sickness, disability, widowhood, old age or other lack of livelihood in circumstances beyond his control. (Article 25) Obviously, some states will be better able to satisfy all the Universal Declaration's aims at once and in a mutually sound context. The following remarks concern this dilemma of universality versus the inevitability and desirability of margins for individual states to determine their policy.

The universality of human rights is relatively easy to justify according to legal normative standards. While the Universal Declaration was originally drafted by about fifty, largely Western states, it was embraced as a 'common standard of achievement' by the rest of the world community during the two UN World Conferences on Human Rights (Tehran 1968 and Vienna 1993). Many human rights are also established in broadly ratified international conventions. Moreover, many human rights may be justified as meeting the rigid standards of international customary law or are even part of binding international law, which renders ratification in conventions unnecessary. The UN Human Rights Committee, which monitors compliance with the International Covenant on Civil and Political Rights (ICCPR) includes among this last category the right to freedom from torture, the right not to be subjected to arbitrary arrest and imprisonment and the right to freedom of conscience.[2] Other rights that also pertain to internationally binding law but exceed the scope of the ICCPR are the right of civilians 'to be spared' in times of war (elaborated in the Fourth Geneva Convention), the right to be protected from genocide, freedom to form unions and the right to food. The universal validity of such rights is not subject to debate, at least not as legal standards.

The debate about the universality of human rights arose in 1992-1993 on the eve of the aforementioned Second UN World Conference on Human Rights. Universality is known to have been asserted most vehemently at the African and Asian regional preparatory meetings in Tunis (1992) and Bangkok (1993), respectively. Together the Asian nations stated: '… while human rights are universal in nature, they must be considered in the context of a dynamic and evolving process of international norm-setting, bearing in mind the significance of national and regional particularities and various historical, cultural and regional backgrounds.' [3]

The Member States of the Organization of the Islamic Conference used similar words – 'taking into account the various historical, cultural and religious backgrounds and the principal legal systems' – in their *Cairo Declaration on Human Rights in Islam.*[4]

The Bangkok Declaration was quoted many times, because according to Western views it directly challenged the absolute and universal validity of human rights.

At the World Conference many speakers addressed the question of universal applicability, including P. Kooijmans, the Dutch Minister of Foreign Affairs at the time. After stating that universality of human rights standards was inherent in the concept of human rights, and that human rights should simply be considered inalienable, Kooijmans submitted that 'only governments sometimes call into question the universality of human rights, not the people, and not the victims of violations.'[5] Thus the potentates are the ones who object to civilians defending their rights and may therefore dredge up the universality theme ('those human rights are a Western invention and are part of Western culture'). Populations, individuals and non-governmental organizations (NGOs), however, rarely propagate such conceptual elasticity. The fact that the North Korean government participates in qualifying such universality while the South Korean government does not ('what differences in culture?') illustrates Kooijmans' idea beautifully.

'Only governments call into question the universality of human rights,' according to Kooijmans. At the World Conference Kooijmans' remarks were given an immediate follow-up by the Chinese delegation leader Liu Huaqui:

> *The concept of human rights is a product of historical development. It is closely associated with specific social, political and economic conditions and the specific history, culture and values of a particular country ... Different historical development stages have different human rights requirements. Countries at different development stages or with different*

historical traditions and cultural backgrounds also have a different under-
standing and practice of human rights.[6]

The Chinese government stated that it had a 'different understanding and practice of human rights'. As we know, the Vienna conference culminated in a statement recognizing the Universal Declaration of Human Rights once again as 'a common standard of achievement for all peoples and all nations', (terminology from the Universal Declaration), and as a 'source of inspiration', ending with the familiar phrases that 'the universal nature of these rights and freedoms is beyond question', and that 'the promotion and protection of all human rights is a legitimate concern of the international community'. The qualifying sentence that 'national and regional particularities and various historical, cultural and religious backgrounds must be borne in mind' is followed immediately by the observation that states have an obligation to protect all human rights, regardless of their political, economic and cultural systems.

What is the value of such statements? I believe that the participants in the Vienna conference were looking for incantations, and that words are only words. The course of events since the World Conference has revealed that – as was to be expected – the agreed formulas lend themselves to a variety of interpretations, and that universality is by no means 'beyond question'. 'Legitimate concern' is another source of confusion and has certainly not lost any of its ambiguity since the World Conference, no matter how widely the words from the conference in Vienna are used in international and bilateral contacts to emphasize the concern's legitimacy. In other words, something has changed since Vienna (in this respect the conference is a link in a long chain), albeit not to the extent that the words chosen suggest.

So much for the negative aspects. On a more positive note, the approach selected conveys a realistic perspective and an attitude compatible with the 'margin of appreciation' mentioned in human rights circles. This margin concerns the freedom of action and policy that states deserve in regard to human rights, with respect to both the substance of many standards and their immediate realization. One such case in Europe, for example, is the admission of countries such as Ukraine and the Russian Federation to the Council of Europe and consequently to the European Convention on the Protection of Human Rights and Fundamental Freedoms. Such large countries with such a wealth of human rights problems will obviously not meet the standards drafted in Strasbourg immediately. Nonetheless, both the Parliamentary Assembly and the Council of Europe's Committee of Ministers have advised and approved their admission, respectively, on the premise that the Strasbourg instruments will promote human rights in these countries. Overall, European history – since the establishment of the modern sovereign states – has shown that realizing human rights is a gradual process that will take a long time and may never be fully accomplished. The generalizations here apply far more specifically as well. In their judicial and semi-judicial actions, international agencies monitoring human rights often grant some latitude to countries where human rights practice is under evaluation, provided these countries respect certain restrictions.

I will not cover the legal details of the 'margin of appreciation' here, but will provide a few examples.[7] 'There is no such thing as a little torture', is the catch phrase in the debate about universality and relativity. I agree, although some situations are not clear-cut. (Should an individual who knows about a bomb set to explode in a residential neighbourhood within minutes be subjected to treatment actually prohibited as torture?) And what about the reasonable term in the justice system or the right to an impartial trial? While the principle underlying the rule at issue is usually clear in such cases, states are often allowed considerable policy freedom either because they deserve it, or because it is the only realistic approach. If a state's government notifies an international supervisory body that it is unable to guarantee a fair trial for lack of the necessary judicial apparatus, but that infrastructure reforms will change the situation in a decade or two, the state will 'be off the hook'. I approve of such latitude, under the stipulation that the state concerned proves that it has no other option at the moment. Regardless of other factors that might come to mind, this practice is commonplace at international judicial and semi-judicial forums.

Let me return to the political debate about the universality of human rights. Here, too, differences in values are often invoked, along with (often in the same breath) requests for understanding for problems that countries encounter in establishing human rights. One such case is the frequently quoted argument that the Indonesian Minister of Foreign Affairs A. Alatas raised at the Vienna conference. The following quotation is long but nevertheless most enlightening:

> ... while we in the developing world do understand and appreciate the genesis of the thinking and motivation underlying present-day Western policies and views on human rights, we should at least expect similar understanding and appreciation of the historical formation and experiences of non-Western societies and the attendant development of our cultural and social values and traditions. For many developing countries, some endowed with ancient and highly developed cultures, have not gone through the same history and experience as the Western nations in developing their ideas on human rights and democracy. In fact, they often developed different perceptions based on different experiences regarding the relations between man and society, man and his fellow man and regarding the rights of the community as against the rights of the individual. In saying so, it is not my intention to therefore propose a separate or alternative concept of human rights. But this is a call for greater recognition of the immense complexity of the issue of human rights due to the wide diversity in history, culture, value systems, geography and phases of development among the nations of the world. [8]

There are two possible responses to arguments like the one presented by Alatas. One is to reject them on the ground that Alatas represents a country that achieved economic success under an authoritarian regime, where the government had every reason to evade the clutches of 'human rights criticism'. Alternatively, Alatas' argument may be justified, and perhaps he is right that the West should be somewhat less rigid about its views and give more consideration to the different contexts in which human rights standards need to be realized. I support a combination of the two responses: avoid invoking 'particularities' as a pretext for escaping criticism, and keep an open mind towards other genuine insights and problems. Such a modifying approach need not mean sacrificing principles, as is often maintained. On the contrary, the objective is to elevate the debate on universality above the level of slogans that characterized the East-West relationship and has been surfacing lately in the relationships between North and South and between Islamic and non-Islamic states. Communicating in slogans will not lead to a substantive debate. A bit more relativism from the West is therefore welcome, along with loyal support for fundamental human rights, emphasizing the need for gradual expansion of the core list of rights and receptiveness to other approaches where justifiable on solid grounds. Neither the 'core list' nor the 'solid grounds' concepts have been standardized yet. Rather, these ongoing debates will require a lot of time to resolve.

The human rights standards to be achieved are thus generally clear, as is the need to allow states some freedom in setting policy. Next, the discussion can focus on the means that are or should be available to the international community to promote their realization. Over time, various mechanisms have been devised in the international arena (United Nations) and in the different regional networks (Council of Europe, Organization for Security and Cooperation in Europe (OSCE), Organization of African Unity, Organization of American States) that further the achievement of human rights. Examples include the various UN human rights conventions with their committees of independent experts, the UN Human Rights Commission with its representatives of member-states, the European Convention on the Protection of Human Rights and Fundamental Freedoms, the Vienna and Moscow supervisory mechanisms of the OSCE etc. These procedures and mechanisms highlight human rights as such. My contribution, however, is not about these specific human rights instruments. The question here is whether linkage with economic relations is a feasible and desirable way of promoting human rights achievement.

The World Trade Organization

Should economic relations be a weapon in the struggle against human rights violations? This is one of the many facets of the conditionality issue. The demand for a conditional approach to economics and human rights ('we will trade with you, if you meet various human rights conditions') has become widespread in recent years. One such case involves the World Trade Organization, which was established in 1994 and today has over 130 member-states. Should this organization exclude countries that prohibit trade unions or sell products manufactured by slave labour on the free world market? This situation is known as the 'social clause'. Although the concept's exact substance is not yet fully defined, it is beginning to take shape. Its essence encompasses freedom to form trade unions, the right to collective bargaining, the elimination of exploitative child labour, prohibition of forced labour and an end to discrimination in employment.[9] Over the years (1930-1973), these standards have gained recognition in seven conventions of the International Labour Organization (ILO), which are also called core conventions or human rights conventions. They cover forced labour (convention No. 29); freedom of association and protection of the right to organize (87); the right to organize and collective bargaining convention (98); the equal remuneration convention (100); the abolition of forced labour convention (105); discrimination (the employment and occupation convention, 111); and the minimum age convention (138). By the end of February 2000 these conventions were ratified by over a hundred (128-152) states, except the treaty on child labour, which was ratified by 84 states.[10] This last figure makes the convention on a minimum working age the most controversial of the lot. The lack of ratifications is attributable to the serious differences of opinion on child labour: there is no agreement worldwide on abolishing child labour as such, but only on the elimination of the most exploitative forms. On this issue, the ILO adopted the Convention Concerning the Prohibition and Immediate Elimination of the Worst Forms of Child Labour in June 1999.[11] At the beginning of the new millennium, we are waiting for a considerable number of ratifications of the Convention to ensure that it will be seen as part of the social clause.

At present, the social clause consists of rights that are universally applicable to some degree. This composition is apparent from the text adopted at the Social Summit of March 1995 in Copenhagen, which stated that governments should improve the quality of work by respecting the aforementioned ILO conventions. Moreover, these conventions also apply in countries that have not ratified them.[12] Extending the legal scope of the concerned ILO conventions beyond the ratifying states enhances their worldwide validity, especially considering that 185 states participated in the Copenhagen conference.[13] Thus, the universal applicability of the social clause's core standards is no longer open to question. This is even truer since the adoption by the ILO of the Declaration on Fundamental Principles and Rights at Work in 1998. In this Declaration, all ILO members agree to observe the 'human rights conventions' of the ILO, even if they have not ratified them.[14]

Enforcing these standards is an entirely different matter. In the past the WTO has received several requests to provide some form of supervision. In December 1996, however, the WTO Conference of Ministers (the organization's highest body), decided to entrust enforcement to the ILO.[15] This arrangement is little more than a draft agreement. What will happen if the ILO condemns the practices of a WTO member remains unclear. Will this state's membership be suspended, or can the WTO take action against the state concerned? The details need to be elaborated. Nor is it clear to what extent satisfying the social clause will be a condition for joining the WTO. The debates over the accession of the People's Republic of China illustrate the situation. In 1948 the country joined GATT (the predecessor of the WTO) but withdrew after the communist take-over in 1949. In 1986 China tried unsuccessfully to join again.[16] By now agreement appears to be growing regarding China's accession to the WTO, and the terms of accession form the main subject of debate.

I believe that prospective WTO members should at least have ratified the aforementioned core conventions of the ILO (with the possible exception of Convention 138) at the time of their accession. Countries like China have a long way to go, as among the conventions mentioned China has ratified only No. 111 on discrimination. Otherwise, aspiring members should agree to abide by the decisions of the different supervisory ILO bodies. Suspension of WTO membership should be an option in the event of persistent defiance (possibly for a five-year term). As stated, no agreements have been reached on this subject.

Clearly, the 'recruitment' of the ILO means opting for the organization's system of enforcing the fundamental labour standards. The emphasis will be on voluntary compliance with the agreements reached, dialogue, tripartism (employers, employees and governments are represented throughout the ranks of the ILO), social support and the absence of judicial coercion and sanctions. Assigning the social clause to the ILO therefore signifies accepting the methods that have established the ILO and its reputation.

As for whether I approve of these methods, I will limit myself here to a general conclusion on linking the WTO with human rights: in the WTO we should not argue in favour of a complete link between human rights observance and access to the free world market. Free access to the world market should, in my view, be contingent only on human rights that are directly related to the production process and are largely universally applicable. The first criterion is based on the idea that non-compliance might provide the violating state with a competitive edge and thus automatically lies within the jurisdiction of the WTO. The rights should also be universally applicable to avert an ongoing debate about the standard's universality rather than its implementation. This line of argument brings me to the human rights conventions of the ILO listed above. States interested in participating in the WTO may be expected to ratify the ILO conventions (e.g. the five aforementioned core rights) and to allow the ILO to monitor their compliance, on pain of measures to be determined (see above).

This agenda seems rather modest. First, it is not a static entity. Standards that are not yet universal (such as the prohibition of child labour), may become part of the core of universal, fundamental labour standards within a few decades. Careful consideration of the fundamental labour standards already selected reveals that together they cover a very broad scope. Freedom to form trade unions, for example, aside from its intrinsic value, has major ramifications regarding freedom of association and assembly and freedom of expression. Moreover, participation in the WTO opens new doors that were closed for various reasons until recently. The information agreement established within the WTO in February/March 1997 is a case in point. This agreement covers services such as telex and fax communication and mobile and personal communication services and systems.[17] Countries joining this agreement will have increasing difficulty preventing the free exchange of information. Thus, what cannot be enforced via the official human rights channels will be accomplished via the back door.

The EC/EU

The EC/EU is the second major forum where conditionality is an ongoing issue of consideration. The wealth of policy documents and convention texts, drafted over the course of a few decades, depicts the EC/EU as an organization with an impressive record of linking trade with respect for human rights. Regarding the operation of such general policy principles, the following two examples illustrate EC/EU policy in this area. The first one concerns the General System of Preferences that the EC/EU has had since 1971, which provides for advantageous export tariffs for developing countries. Under this system's provisions, additional preferences may be assigned to countries observing ILO conventions 87, 98 and 138 (see above).[18] The preference system also provides opportunities for investigating violations of relevant ILO conventions and imposing penalties accordingly. Following its investigation of working conditions in Burma (Myanmar), for example, the European Commission revoked this country's preferences with respect to industrial and agricultural products.[19] In addition, a complaint lodged by the International Confederation of Free Trade Unions and the European Trade Union Confederation (which both initiated the procedure against Burma as well) has given rise to a similar investigation against Pakistan.[20]

The second case concerns the human rights clauses that the EC/EU currently includes in bilateral treaties. Whereas the Baltic clause – an explicit suspension clause authorizing the suspension of the application of the agreement in whole or in part with 'immediate effect' in cases of a serious breach of essential provisions[21] – used to be commonplace, the Bulgarian clause has been standard practice since October 1992. This general, non-execution clause provides for appropriate measures should the parties fail to meet their obligations, following a consultation procedure (except in case of special urgency).[22] According to the European Commission:

> *The difference between the two formulas resides in the degree of sensitivity allowed for. The 'Baltic clause' is more severe in that it provides only for extreme cases warranting immediate suspension without consultation of any kind. The 'Bulgarian clause' not only provides for a consultation procedure and a range of different options but is also designed to keep the*

agreement operational wherever possible. It asserts that immediate suspension should be envisaged only in cases of special urgency. [23]

The Bulgarian clause figures in the agreements with the Russian Federation, Ukraine and Slovakia[24] and in the agreements with several Mediterranean countries (e.g. Israel).[25]

The preceding arrangement suggests that the EC/EU links economic collaboration and human rights through concepts such as positive measures, dialogue and cooperation. The main idea is therefore to reward good behaviour and to keep economic and political dialogue going until results are forthcoming. This conduct is apparently the best way for states to get along. I further believe that from a human rights perspective this method will be the most fruitful in the long run.[26]

On the other hand, the EC/EU – unlike the ILO – has far more powerful instruments besides the opportunities for dialogue. Cases in point are the resolutions of condemnation submitted to the UN Human Rights Commission (a deceptively modest instrument that can achieve a powerful impact), freezing financial assets, revoking preferential status and total discontinuation of economic collaboration. Because of the requirement that decision-making on resolutions under the Common Foreign and Security Policy (CFSP) be unanimous, the most substantial instruments available to the current fifteen members of the European Union are rather theoretical, unless countries with little power commit extremely serious violations.

Aside from the difficulty of implementing serious measures, a tough approach has several drawbacks. Economic isolation often exacerbates internal contradictions and leads to rising repression of a population that is already suffering. Ultimately, those who were supposed to receive assistance are the victims of the serious measures. Accordingly, the EC/EU has performed 'bypass' operations in many bilateral economic and development relations. If economic cooperation with the authorities proves impossible because the government is ineffective (the 'failed states'), corrupt or uses monies received to expand the state apparatus, collaboration will often be through non-government channels. NGOs maintain direct contact with the core of society, which is in turn revitalized by this method.

Human Rights as a Commodity: Conclusions

Countries do not, as such, actually violate 'human rights', as journalistic turns of phrase tend to suggest. Nonetheless, human rights violations are widespread in some countries. While the distinction appears subtle, the formulation reveals a vast difference. The first assertion provides only a global impression of everything that is wrong, whereas the second one calls for a precise indication of the rights that are at stake. The same argument applies to the question as to whether human rights are universally valid. Human rights cover a broad scope and do not necessarily satisfy the rigid criteria of 'universal applicability' in all cases. Hard evidence is needed as described at the beginning of this chapter and elaborated with respect to several fundamental labour rights in the section on the WTO.

Determining how a right may be considered universally applicable is inextricably linked with the issue of whether states are willing to accept the universal value of these fundamental rights as the principle of their actions. Consider the Asian commentary on universality, as presented in the first section of this contribution. Partial agreement with the Asian criticism does not preclude support for the universal core of the human rights idea, as I have argued. Nor is the unilateral imposition of human rights on these countries useful at this point. International political relations will obstruct such an approach. This situation underlies my argument regarding the 'social clause'. I believe that countries wishing to enjoy the benefits of WTO membership need to observe several defined and carefully circumscribed rights. These rights, however, are not imposed as a unilateral dictate but are presented as a contract to be observed according to the regulations of the WTO and the ILO.

Rights other than the ones elaborated above should not be linked with access to world trade in my view. All too easily, cliché-like associations arise between respect for human rights and trade relations based on the idea that something needs to be done about countries that permit widespread torture or prohibit freedom of the press. Although the intention certainly appeals to me, trade relations are not necessarily the right instrument for promoting such rights. Often, threatening the use of sanctions seems more like a Pavlovian reaction than a response in which the party advocating economic measures provides reasonable proof that this instrument will lead to improvement.

If the instrument cannot reasonably be related to the effect, trade relations should not be used to this end – at least not in a negative sense. What remains is an emphasis on positive measures: positive conditionality (see my statements above on the method of the ILO and the EC/EU). While many of those in human rights circles will find this conclusion less than satisfactory, it may be the only reasonable option.

Parts of this contribution were published previously in: W.J.M. van Genugten, 'Universele gelding van mensenrechten en (de grenzen aan) het recht van bemoeienis van de internationale gemeenschap', in Y. Broer *et al.*, Eds. (1995). *Mensenrechten in Zuidoost-Azië: geijkte machteloosheid of nieuw beleid* (proceedings of the symposium with the same name). Utrecht; W.J.M. van Genugten (1997). *WTO, ILO en EG: handelen in vrijheid.* Deventer: Tjeenk Willink.

NOTES

1. EC (European Community) signifies the first pillar of the Maastricht Treaty. It concerns the activities that were traditionally the core of European cooperation. EU (European Union) represents the second and third pillars, concerning the Common Foreign and Security Policy and cooperation in justice and home affairs, respectively. This contribution uses EC/EU to cover both elements.
2. The complete list of the Human Rights Committee reads: 'The right to engage in slavery, to torture, to subject persons to cruel, inhuman or degrading treatment or punishment, to arbitrarily deprive persons of their lives, to arbitrarily arrest and detain persons, to deny freedom of thought, conscience and religion, to presume a person guilty unless he proves his innocence, to execute pregnant women and children, to permit the advocacy of national, racial or religious hatred, to deny to persons of marriageable age the right to marry, or to deny to minorities the right to enjoy their own culture, profess their own religion, or use their own language, and ... the right to a fair trial ....' See the 'General Comment' of the Human Rights Committee of November 1994 (ICCPR/C/21/Rev.1/Add.6).
3. Bangkok Declaration, A/CONF.157/ASRM/7, Par. 8.
4. The Declaration was adopted in Cairo on 5 August 1990. The decision to submit it as a 'position paper' to the World Conference was taken at a meeting a meeting of the ministers of Foreign Affairs of the Islamic nations in Karachi on 25-29 April 1993.
5. Speech of 14 June 1993.
6. Speech of 15 June 1993.

7. See, for example, J.G.C. Schokkenbroek, 'De Margin of Appreciation-doctrine in de jurisprudentie van het Europese Hof', in A.W. Heringa, J.G.C. Schokkenbroek and J. van der Velde, Eds. (1990). *40 Jaar Europees Verdrag voor de Rechten van de Mens.* Leiden: NJCM.

8. Speech of 14 June 1993.

9. Lower House, The Hague, 1996-1997, 25074, No. 1, p. 10; R. Torres, 'Labour Standards and Trade', in *The OECD Observer*, 1996, 10-12; on the OECD report: *Trade, Employment and Labour Standards: A Study of Core Workers' Rights and International Trade.* Paris: OECD, 1996; *Sociaal-Economische Raad, Fundamentele arbeidsnormen en internationale handel.* The Hague: SER, 1996, pp. 14-17.

10. According to a report by the Applications of Standards Branch of the International Labour Standards Department of the ILO, February 2000.

11. Published in *International Legal Materials*, Washington DC: The American Society of International Law, 1999, pp. 1207-1214.

12. Copenhagen Programme of Action, March 1995, Par. 54.

13. Lower House, The Hague, 1994-1995, 23900 XV, No. 42, p. 2.

14. Published in *International Legal Materials*, 1233, Washington DC: The American Society of International Law, (1998), p. 1237.

15. Yeo Cheow Tong, 'Concluding Remarks by the Chairman: We have delivered', in *WTO Focus*, No. 15, January 1997, p. 14.

16. 'The World Trade Organization and the European Community', *Working Paper of the European Parliament.* Luxembourg: The European Parliament, 1995, p. 49.

17. Lower House, The Hague, 1996-1997, 25074, No. 5, p. 1.

18. A.W. van der Klaauw, 'Mensenrechten en ontwikkelingsbeleid van de Europese Gemeenschap', in *NJCM Bulletin*, 1997, 22, 10; COM (95) 567 def., p. 26; COM (96) 402 def., p. 14.

19. Van der Klaauw, *op. cit.*, pp. 10-11. For more information about the backgrounds, see: CES 240/98; advice from the Economic and Social Committee of the EC/EU about the 'Voorstel voor een verordening (EG) van de Raad houdende tijdelijke intrekking van de voordelen van het aan de Unie van Myanmar toegekende stelsel van algemene tariefpreferenties voor industrieproducten' and also regarding 'agricultural products', February 1997, *passim.*

20. Cf.: Van der Klaauw, *op. cit.*, p. 11 and CES 240/97, pp. 4-5, as well as additional oral reports from officials at the Economic and Social Committee in Brussels.

21. COM (95) 216 def., p. 8.

22. *Ibid.*, p. 8 and 10.

23. *Ibid.*, p. 8.

24. *Ibid.*

25. Lower House, The Hague, 1996-1997, 25036, No. 1 ff.

26. See, for example, W.J.M. van Genugten, 'Toelating tot de Raad van Europa: "acquis" op de tocht of gepaste rekkelijkheid?', in *Nederlands Juristenblad*, 1996, 7, pp. 249-251.

H. Hazelzet

Hadewych Hazelzet obtained a Masters of Arts from the University of Chicago *cum laude* in 1996. The title of her thesis was *The Price of Morality in International Trade: Towards a Just Trade Theory*. Afterwards she worked as a research assistant for the Analysis and Forecasting Unit of the UNESCO in Paris and for a consultancy firm in Utrecht. She is currently conducting doctoral research on economic sanctions and human rights at the European University Institute in Florence. During the winter of 1999-2000 she worked as the assistant to the EU Economic and Financial Sanctions Co-ordinator at the European Commission in Brussels.

7

THE PRICE OF JUST TRADE MEASURES

The Sanctions Against Iraq

Hadewych Hazelzet

Newspapers and international forums abound with calls for trade measures, sanctions and withdrawal of investments from countries where human rights are violated. The cause is noble but all too easily invoked in the name of justice. When the Dutch Minister of Foreign Affairs Van Mierlo took a firm stand against China, however, a backlash of criticism resulted.[1] The reproaches came largely from corporate industry and governments with the strongest financial interest in smooth trade relations, such as France's Airbus.[2] The consequences of the proposed measures underwent little or no systematic investigation and elaboration. Major multinationals, such as Shell, have responded to ongoing criticism from society at large by calling for analytical frameworks to provide a basis for systematic consideration of ethical dilemmas in international trade.[3] This contribution offers a perspective on practices in international trade to help evaluate whether potential measures are justified. The question as to who is 'right' and who is 'wrong' is less relevant for the moment. The main question is: what are morally justifiable reasons for intervening in another country's economy, and, if a trade relationship exists, which codes of conduct are morally justifiable for governments and businesses?

Although both governments and businesses face ethical issues in international trade, governments are the main focus in this contribution. After all, if governments prohibit trade with a certain country, businesses will have no say in the matter. Only if trade takes place with the country's businesses can ethical dilemmas arise regarding international investments and production processes. Thus far, trade measures are assessed almost exclusively according to their effectiveness (determined on the basis of desired policy changes)[4] and not according to the principle and ethical dilemmas underlying the measures to be implemented. How should we interpret the differences in the severity of the conditions imposed on trade relations with countries that violate human rights? In this contribution I attribute these differences to the way countries weigh their interest in trade with the country concerned and the degree of moral indignation over human rights violations there. The more the moral indignation exceeds self-interest, the more serious the conditions imposed and vice versa. In these cases, the degree of moral indignation can be determined by the price that the country stating the conditions is willing to pay for impeding trade. Businesses deciding whether to invest in such countries face similar dilemmas.

After considering this decision, I will address crucial questions that may provide a solution to ethical dilemmas in international trade. The usefulness of this so-called Just Sanctions Doctrine is determined according to the dilemmas raised by the extreme trade measures against Iraq.

Trade and Ethics

Why are ethical aspects of trade eliciting so much attention at present? There are various explanations. International trade has skyrocketed since the end of World War II. Only toward the end of the Cold War did this trend change the nature of international relations as well. While previously military weapons had been used to punish another country's conduct, economic measures have become far more popular.[5] Trade measures are much less costly and require fewer sacrifices by the public. Greater dependence on each other for trade enables countries to do serious damage through trade measures. Businesses are forced to consider the ethical aspects of trading as well.[6] Modern communication methods inform people about the political and economic conditions under which their consumer goods are manufactured. The electorate that demands trade measures from the government also votes with its wallet on the products it consumes.[7]

Increased trade is making the borders between states less pronounced. The limits of the responsibility of manufacturers, consumers and governments are similarly difficult to identify. Who has a clear conscience, and who is guilty? The manufacturers offering products of dubious origin, the consumers buying them, or the governments allowing such products into their country? Fingers are pointed in all directions, as everyone hides behind each other and hopes somebody else will provide an answer. What can our tiny country, a single business or the average consumer's purchasing power change about situations where human rights are violated?

Statements

Bluntly stated, governments, businesses and consumers will follow through on their noble intentions only if the cost of fair trade is not excessive. This observation underlies the following statements.

a. No trade: moral indignation prevails

The greater the moral indignation over human rights violations, the greater the willingness to pay the price and the more severe the measures taken. Examples include the sanctions against Iraq, South Africa, Rhodesia and Serbia. Often, the moral indignation is virtually universal in that the measures are enforced by the United Nations. Most of these measures target authoritarian regimes.

b. Free trade: economic and political interests prevail

The greater the importance of trade with the country concerned, or the greater the preference for or dependence on that country's products, the higher the cost of suspending trade. Such action means a political sacrifice for governments enacting the trade measures and a financial sacrifice for domestic consumers and producers. The sanctions will require that less efficient producers be used and will increase the product's price. The domestic producers affected will blame the government and exert pressure, while other businesses will benefit. Thus, the greater the political and financial sacrifice associated with trade restrictions, the less likely that trade will be subject to conditions. The Netherlands will be loath to decree trade measures against Germany, its chief trading partner, if this country commits immoral actions in the international system of states. This category is illustrated by the relatively unrestricted trade between member-states of free-trade agreements such as the EU. Most of these cases involve trade between democracies.[8]

c. Conditioned trade: both economic and political importance and moral indignation

Between the extremes mentioned above from unconditional trade to a total trade embargo lies a large grey area. If the country concerned is both economically and politically important, and has provoked moral indignation, the measures are usually half-hearted.[9] In these vague situations the different parties are especially likely to hide behind each other. Acquiring a grasp of such common and tricky situations is essential for devising ethically sound policy. In this grey area countries take their own trade measures, which are not adopted by other countries. Unilateral measures may be perceived as being more subjective than multilateral measures with international support. One relevant case concerns the disagreement mentioned above that arose within the European Union in April 1997, when the Dutch presidency tried to submit a resolution against China to the UN Human Rights Commission in Geneva. France – which had just returned from a trade mission to China – refused to jeopardize its trade interests. Spain, Italy and Germany followed suit. Likewise, the United States threatens to revoke China's Most Favored Nation status every year. Other measures taken by the United States on moral grounds, regardless of international support from other states, include sanctions against countries that they feel are not doing enough in the 'war on drugs' (e.g. Colombia) or the trade embargo against Cuba, imposed to express disapproval of Castro's communist regime. Nigeria's share in the global oil market enabled the country to get away with only diplomatic sanctions when various human rights activists were hung there in 1995.[10] Trade measures in this grey area usually concern regimes that tread a fine line between a token democracy and a dictatorship.

Obviously, differences in political and economic power are important: countries can take trade measures against a small country like Colombia out of dissatisfaction with its drug policy more easily and more effectively than vice versa. Some countries in the grey zone that were considered Third World nations until recently are now trying to enforce their economic and political power (and are therefore able to avoid heavy trade sanctions). China sets the tone by using its sales and investment market to protect itself from threats by trade partners.[11]

The statements reveal a sliding scale in the measure of self-interest and moral indignation, in combinations that lead to no trade, conditioned trade or free trade.[12] The more moral indignation prevails over self-interest, the more rigid are the restrictions on the trade relationship. Other motives reflecting rising degrees of moral indignation occur as well: 'to be neutral'/'promote affluence' (free trade), 'to promote good' (trade subject to positive conditions often associated with aid), 'to prevent harm' (trade subject to negative conditions) and 'to punish evil' (no trade).[13]

The Just Sanctions Doctrine

How can we judge trade measures allegedly taken on moral grounds? And how do we determine whether to use trade measures (and if so which type) to punish countries that violate human rights? We need a list of guidelines for dealing with the dilemmas that inevitably arise with human rights violations and trade repercussions. Depending on the specific situation, these dilemmas call for a justified response to enable appropriate measures to be taken.

In the military context, there are already ethical guidelines for determining whether military intervention is justified. These guidelines also stipulate how soldiers should behave when they do intervene to avoid committing war crimes and is known as the Just War Doctrine.[14] This doctrine is considered a voluntary imposition of internationally recognized justifications for entering war (*jus ad bellum*) and codes of conduct during war (*jus in bello*). It provides a basis for ethical evaluations of war practices.

Theoretically, the Just War Doctrine approach to war strikes a balance between the concepts known as realism and pacifism in international relations. Realists assert that war is a hell that obliterates all forms of morality.[15] Pacifists advise abstaining from all violent activity, even if peace may be unjust.[16] Finally, the Just War tradition pursues ways to maintain standards and principles, even during war.[17] Elshtain explains: 'Just war as political theory touches both the deontological and consequentialist poles of moral reasoning. By embracing both dimensions, [it] cuts across the usual lines of faults in moral philosophy just as it does in international relations as political theory by refusing to fit ... inside the realist-idealist dichotomy.'[18] According to deontological moral arguments, certain actions or types of conduct are morally justified by principles, such as references to biblical or humane values. Consequential moral argumentation is based purely on the question of whether the action or conduct has served its purpose and achieved an impact. The Just War tradition derives its arguments and its power from both forms of moral reasoning.

In keeping with this convention, a sanctions convention may be drafted offering guidelines for handling two dilemmas.[19]

1) Which grounds justify economic intervention in another country and trade restrictions? In other words, how might a *jus ad sanctionem* be formulated?

2) If economic relations exist, how should trade partners be expected to behave? What would a *jus in commercio* (i.e. continued trading) be or a *jus in sanctione* (i.e. during sanctions)?

In either extreme (unrestricted trade versus no trade), ethical dilemmas are different from those in the grey area. After all, the more serious the trade measures, the greater the likelihood that the effects on the population will raise ethical questions. The goal is to punish the regime, not the population. The problem is that such regimes rarely care about the population. Whose concern is it when children die as a result of the sanctions against Iraq: that of Saddam Hussein, of the parties imposing the sanctions, or of both sides?

Where trade is unrestricted, justifications seem unnecessary, as the objective is to raise the standard of living. Even in such cases, some countries try to do the right thing, for example by subjecting trade agreements to conditions. The EU is particularly adept at this art: since 1991 nearly all association agreements with third countries include a clause stipulating respect for human rights and requiring that the regime promote democratic processes.[20] Turkey and Eastern Europe receive assistance in meeting these conditions.[21] This approach seems far more promising than isolating a country through penal measures.[22]

The preceding statements indicate that the need for guidelines on *jus in sanctione/commercio* is the most acute where moral indignation is greatest and trade therefore least. Where personal interest in trade and moral indignation are intertwined, however, the demand for a carefully circumscribed *jus ad sanctionem* is greatest. In such cases the measures are often imposed by individual states and are not shared by the international community of states. Here, fine moralistic formulations often cover up self-interest. In this grey area (e.g. China, Colombia, Cuba and Nigeria) ironclad justifications are therefore especially important for economic intervention in another sovereign state.

The Just War Doctrine's guidelines for the Just Sanctions Doctrine to be devised here combine the following deontological and consequential ethical arguments.[23]

Jus ad sanctionem
- Does the party imposing the sanction have the right intention, and is there just cause?
- Are the measures a last resort after all other means have been exhausted?
- What is the probability of success of the measures?
- Are the damage and the cost of the measures proportional to their expected outcome?
- Are the measures decreed by a legitimate and competent authority and supported by a representative share of the population in the country to be affected?
- What is the comparative justice in the arguments of both parties? [24]

Jus in sanctione
- Will these measures be discriminatory toward innocent people?
- Are the damage and the cost of the measures proportional to their expected outcome?

How can such a Just Sanctions doctrine be made operational? To assess the value of the ethical approach advocated here, we will apply the principles stated above to an extreme case of economic intervention: the sanctions against Iraq.[25] These guidelines provide a basis for standard questions in all kinds of situations. Companies with a modicum of creativity will ask themselves the same questions in deciding about their investments in countries where human rights are violated.

The Sanctions Against Iraq

The trade measures against Iraq are to be viewed as extreme measures. Iraq exemplifies the application of the ethical approach advocated above. Economic intervention was easy to justify but gave rise to distressing ethical dilemmas, for example because of the large numbers of children dying of malnutrition every day.[26]

What was the justification for the *jus ad sanctionem*? There was certainly just cause for the sanctions against Iraq. The goal was (a) to punish Iraq for its aggressive invasion of an internationally recognized sovereign state; (b) to punish Iraq for its genocide against the Kurds; (c) to deter the country from repeating such action; and finally – on a more controversial note – (d) to overthrow the Ba'ath regime. Such actions enabled the countries imposing sanctions to keep a clean record and a clear conscience. These countries therefore had clear-cut intentions and a view as how to end the situation.

Moreover, Iraq's arguments were by no means ones of comparative justice. The countries imposing sanctions under the UN mandate were competent and legitimate authorities. Since the Kurdish population was a minority and the society severely repressed, no straightforward method was available to assess the population's support for the sanctions ('competent authority'). The sanctions had not been imposed as a last resort and after exhaustion of all other means, since they coincided with military force.[27] The search for a political solution was quickly abandoned after Hussein's invasion of Kuwait and his manifest unwillingness to cooperate with the effort ('last resort').

The probability of the measures succeeding was less clear. Since the expected outcome did not prove immediately feasible, it is difficult to assess the proportionality of the damage and costs of the measures. This case, however, is more one of *jus in sanctione*. Although the sanctions were intended to incite the population against its non-elected regime, such sentiment was difficult to cultivate. Overall, the reasons for economic intervention in Iraq may be considered just: straightforward arguments are available to support at least four of the six dilemmas.

How can *jus in sanctione* be justified? This task is even more difficult than the *jus ad sanctionem* – but no less important. Who is supposed to care if innocent people suffer from trade measures? Hussein certainly did not seem very concerned about his people, at least not about the Kurds. He was therefore unlikely to behave differently toward them. The sanctions did, however, provide a convenient excuse for him to blame domestic problems on foreign enemies and to incite his people against them.

One of the goals of the sanctions was to deter other countries from similar crimes. From a consequential, ethical perspective, 'prevention of future aggression or genocide' is extremely difficult to assert as a moral standard, since hardly any empirical evidence is available regarding the sanctions' effectiveness in bringing about policy changes or toppling regimes.[28] From a deontological perspective, however, other potentially aggressive regimes might be dissuaded from committing such crimes. The question remains as to whether the Iraqi population should be used as a deterrent. This would violate human dignity, especially since the effect is unclear. Finally, the horrifying question arises as to whether deaths from hunger and malnutrition are preferable to genocide and aggression. Genocide is obviously a crime against humanity and a political community's right to exist. As long as the regime controls access to food, it can find different means to wipe out the population. In these cases, the consequences of the international sanctions violate social and economic rights as a response to an immoral regime's violations of political and cultural rights. Is such a decision morally justifiable?

Neither Hussein nor the countries imposing sanctions offered the population any means to escape the sanctions.[29] Hussein even refused to accept humanitarian aid and food. Only in May 1996 was agreement reached on exchanging oil for aid. Since this effort began, however, hundreds of thousands of Iraqis have become malnourished or ill according to UN estimates.[30] We may therefore place the blame with the leader of the population 'held hostage.' The countries imposing sanctions are guilty as well, since they have an obligation to avert the suffering of innocent victims. Even when hurting the population is inevitable, such action remains a crime.[31] Whether an economic stranglehold as a means of inciting people against their unjust leaders is morally appropriate is unclear: 'It is too closely reminiscent of siege tactics, treating civilian population as hostages, their suffering as a lever.' [32]

Do the sanctions against Iraq reflect a dire emergency, where crimes against the innocent are permitted for the sake of a higher justice? Was the suffering necessary, even though it was most unfortunate and could be viewed as a crime? Should the sanctions continue after a status quo has been reached, or do they go beyond what is just? Walzer believes it would make a difference if a clear majority of the citizens approved of the sanctions and condemned Hussein's policy. If these citizens demonstrated their legitimacy, as the ANC did in South Africa, the international community would be justified in perpetuating the sanctions. The next question is obviously how the Iraqi citizens can manifest their stand. (This problem existed to a lesser degree with the population in Haiti, which had elected the deposed President Aristide by 67 per cent, and in Serbia-Montenegro, where the regime had the support of the public.[33])

Although the sanctions may be considered proportional to the gross injustice of violating international law and human rights, their effect on the population is so tremendous and their success so unlikely that *jus in sanctione* appears to have exceeded the limits of what is morally justifiable. The problem is that the measures do not distinguish between innocent citizens and true criminals, and that Hussein thwarted efforts to provide humanitarian aid. If the international community directed the sanctions more specifically against the true criminals, *jus in sanctione* would be easier to uphold.

The Price of Morality

This contribution was a first step toward an ethical perspective on international trade practices. First, I reviewed the relationship between the costs of trade measures and the degree of moral indignation over the human rights violations versus the severity of possible trade measures. Next, I argued the need for and feasibility of a Just Sanctions Doctrine as a way of coping with the ethical dilemmas elicited by the trade measures.

As the case of Iraq demonstrates, consequential and deontological arguments – which both pertain to the Just Sanctions Doctrine – are important for evaluating whether trade measures are justified. Straightforward policy recommendations in this complex field of ethics and international trade are therefore impossible to provide. The arguments that are decisive for taking certain measures or perpetuating them need to be examined in each case. As a general rule, deontological arguments might prevail over consequential ones in cases of doubt. As Van Luijk explains, the 'general, underlying ethical [i.e. deontological] principle is [...] that demonstrable individual rights carry more moral weight than benefits that offset each other.' [34] In cases where the *jus ad sanctionem* is justified, the *jus in sanctione* often raises serious problems, whereas without due cause for intervention, codes of conduct are even harder to justify. Nonetheless, the analytical distinction between the two appears very worthwhile, both from a theoretical perspective and in deciding whether to impose or continue trade measures and in determining their severity.

No longer can producers, consumers and governments hide behind each other. Nor do companies such as Shell need to answer to the 'squeaky wheel'.[35] At present, both businesses and national social organizations such as Amnesty International and Pax Christi, as well as international organizations such as the OECD and the ILO, are drafting guidelines and codes of conduct for businesses. As these cases involve codes of conduct for trading rather than sanctions, I refer to them as *jus in commercio*. The standard questions presented here (and the principles they comprise) appear less compelling and more broadly applicable and do not diminish the responsibility and liability for verifying the ethical aspects of trade measures. Literature on earmarked aid may be of use in devising additional analytical frameworks and theories for conditioned trade.

During its presidency of the EU, the Netherlands took the vanguard in the debate about the ethical aspects of international trade by advocating a resolution against China in the Human Rights Commission – despite the concurrent risk to its own interests. Since the resolution did not receive European support (because of the divergent economic interests within the EU), it would not have been effective (i.e.

consequential). Nonetheless, the Netherlands kept its own record clean (i.e. a deontological approach). This solidly grounded ethical consideration involving both deontological and consequential arguments provides a means for striking a balance between clergymen and merchants and between moral imperialism and moral relativism. Nonetheless, the greatest challenge to developing and realizing ethically responsible trade remains the price we are all willing to pay for our standards and values.

An earlier version of this contribution appeared in *Internationale Spectator*, The Hague, Vol. 2 (1997), No. 51, pp. 93-99. See also Hadewych Hazelzet, 'Assessing the Suffering from "Successful" Sanctions: an Ethical Approach', in: W.J.M. van Genugten and Gerard A. de Groot, Eds. (1999b). *United Nations Sanctions: Effectiveness and Effects, Especially in the Field of Human Rights: A Multi-disciplinary Approach*. Antwerpen; Groningen: Intersentia.

NOTES

1. In April 1997 the Netherlands tried during its presidency of the European Union to submit a resolution to the Human Rights Commission of the United Nations, in which it condemned the human rights situation in China.
2. In the end Van Mierlo changed his view, while the Danes submitted their own resolution and, like the Netherlands, angered China; see *NRC Handelsblad* 4, 5, 7, 8, 15, 16, 21, 24 April and 15 May 1997. One month later President Clinton extended China's Most Favored Nation status once again; *NRC Handelsblad*, 20 May 1997.
3. C.A.J. Herkströter, CEO of the Koninklijke Nederlandsche Petroleum Maatschappij; *NRC Handelsblad*, 12 October and 28 December 1996.
4. See, for example, David A. Baldwin (1985). *Economic Statecraft*. Princeton, NJ: Princeton University Press; D. Leyton-Brown (1987). *The Utility of International Economic Sanctions*. New York: St. Martin's Press; Lisa L. Martin (1992). *Coercive Cooperation: Explaining Multilateral Economic Sanctions*. Princeton, NJ: Princeton University Press; Gary Clyde Hufbauer, Jeffrey J. Schott, and Kimberly Ann Elliott (1985). *Economic Sanctions Reconsidered: History and Current Policy*. Washington DC: Institute for International Economics; S. Rozemond, Ed. (1988). *Economische sancties*. The Hague: Nederlands Instituut voor Internationale Betrekkingen Clingendael. (P.A.G. van Bergeijk's contribution 'Kosten en baten van economische sancties' is an exception to the one-sided focus on the effects of sanctions. He asserts that: 'In my view actions that lead to damages require general and moral justification,' p. 29. He does not elaborate on this remark.)

5. Since the 1960s and especially since the late 1970s, trade measures have come into increasing use as a means of punishing those violating international law. The UN has imposed sanctions on Rhodesia, South Africa, Iraq, Yugoslavia, Somalia, Libya, Liberia, Haiti and Angola. See Sonja Licht, 'The Use of Sanctions in Former Yugoslavia: Can they Assist in Conflict Resolution?', in David Cortright and George A. Lopez, Eds. (1995). *Economic Sanctions: Panacea or Peacebuilding in a post-Cold War World?* Boulder, CO: Westview Press, pp. 153-160; Susan L. Woodward, 'The Use of Sanctions in Former Yugoslavia: Misunderstanding Political Realities', in Cortright and Lopez, *op. cit.*; Lori Fisler Damrosch, 'The Collective Enforcement of International Norms through Economic Sanctions', in *Ethics and International Affairs*, Vol. 8 (1994), 60, pp. 59-75. Over two-thirds of the sanctions imposed between 1945 and 1990 (which amounted to more than sixty) came from the United States. See George A. Lopez and David Cortright, 'Economic Sanctions in Contemporary Global Relations', in Cortright and Lopez, *op. cit.*, pp. 3-16; Hufbauer, Schott and Kimberly, *op. cit.*, pp. 13-20.

6. Multinationals are increasingly starting to contemplate ethical codes of conduct of their own. Heineken withdrew from Burma, Nike is coping with negative publicity regarding working conditions at its factories in Indonesia. In the autumn of 1996 the president of Shell urged social debate following bloodshed in Nigeria. South Africa's apartheid regime no longer exists. Other companies (e.g. The Body Shop, The Gap and Levi Strauss) have been trying to balance profits and principles for years. In April 1997 several major US clothing and shoe manufacturers (e.g. Reebok, Nike, Liz Claiborne and L.L. Bean) agreed to improve working conditions at their factories in the Third World (*NRC Handelsblad*, 15 April 1997).

7. Many consumers seem to be taking a stand. Some refused to purchase petrol from Shell during the incidents in Nigeria or the Brent Spar; others rejected French wine when France was conducting nuclear testing and have boycotted carpets made by child labour.

8. Trade restrictions also arise from many other, sometimes protectionist, motives. My focus here is exclusively on trade restricted on principled grounds in response to human rights violations.

9. In some cases of severe moral indignation, extreme measures are waived out of consideration for the short- and long-term impact that disrupting the economy would have on observance of human rights.

10. 'Nigeria foaming', *The Economist*, London, 18 November 1995, pp. 15-16; 'After the hangings', *The Economist*, London, 18 November 1995, p. 41; European Commission. *Bulletin of the European Union*. Luxembourg: Office for Official Publications of the European Communities, 1995, No. 10, p. 11.

11. China called off the visit by a Dutch trade delegation headed by Minister Wijers of Economic Affairs because of criticism expressed by Minister Van Mierlo of Foreign Affairs as the EU president regarding the observance of human rights in April 1997. *NRC Handelsblad*, 15 April 1997.

12. A more detailed explanation and definition of concepts appears in Hadewych A. Hazelzet (1996). *The Price of Morality in International Trade: Towards a Just*

Trade Theory. Chicago, IL: Committee on International Relations, University of Chicago, ms., pp. 20-24. I view free trade as unregulated trade or trade according to the WTO regulations and regional free-trade agreements. Such trade serves primarily to raise the standard of living. Conditioned trade includes trade agreements comprising social clauses, in which grants are contingent upon, or conditions are included such as 'sustainably produced'/'not produced by child labour'. Thus, trade is intended to promote wellbeing and sustainable development. Sanctions do not ordinarily cover all trade, as a boycott or blockade would. Brady defines sanctions as follows: 'Sanctions are no more than one form of economic denial, in which an existing rather than a potential benefit is denied the target country in response to unacceptable conduct in the international community.' J.D. Brady, 'Utility of Economic Sanctions as a Policy Instrument', in Leyton-Brown, *op. cit.*, p. 297. Nincic and Wallensteen add that 'in order to force the target country to act in a manner that conforms more closely to the initiator's preferences and interests, economic pain will be imposed.' Miroslav Nincic and Peter Wallensteen (1983). *Dilemmas of Economic Coercion: Sanctions in World Politics.* New York: Praeger, p. 4. In this respect the absence of Most Favored Nation status may also be viewed as a sanction. No trade at all means a boycott or blockade. This is the most serious type of economic measure and usually coincides with military intervention.

13. Hazelzet (1996), *op. cit.*, p. 20, offers a metaphor for this analytical distinction. This hypothesis identifies the different types of conditioned trade to understand when which types of trade measures are used without judging which type of measure would be more or less justified or effective in a given situation.

14. Michael Walzer (1977, 2nd edn. 1992). *Just and Unjust Wars: A Moral Argument with Historical Illustrations.* New York: Basic Books; Jean Bethke Elshtain, Ed. (1992). *Just War Theory.* New York: New York University Press; Robert L. Holmes (1989). *On War and Morality.* Princeton, NJ: Princeton University Press; Drew Christiansen and G.F. Powers, 'Economic Sanctions and the Just War Doctrine', in Cortright and Lopez, *op. cit.*, pp. 97-120.

15. See the work by the realists Machiavelli, Hobbes and Thucydides. Hans J. Morgenthau and Kenneth W. Thompson (6th edn. 1993). *Politics among Nations: The Struggle for Power and Peace.* New York: McGraw-Hill; Kenneth N. Waltz (1979). *Theory of International Politics.* Reading, MA: Addison Wesley.

16. See the work by the pacifists Gandhi and Hauerwas. Stanley Hauerwas, 'On Surviving Justly: Ethics and Nuclear Disarmament', in Elshtain, *op. cit.*; Stanley Hauerwas, 'A Pacifist Response to the Bishops', in Paul Ramsey (1988). *Speak up for Just War or Pacifism: A Critique of the United Methodist Bishops' Pastoral Letter 'In Defense of Creation'.* University Park, PA: Pennsylvania State University Press; Robert L. Holmes, *op. cit.*

17. See the work by the Just War theoreticians: Saint Augustine. *The City of God,* London: Penguin Books, 1984; Elshtain, *op. cit.*; James Turner Johnson, 'Threats, Values and Defense: Does the Defense of Values by Force Remain a Moral Possibility?', in Elshtain, *op. cit.*; the Convention of American Catholic Bishops: Catholic Bishops US, 'The Challenge of Peace: God's Promise and our Response: The Pastoral Letter on War and Peace', in Elshtain, *op. cit.*; Paul

Ramsey, 'The Just War Doctrine According to Augustine', in Elshtain, *op. cit.*; Michael Walzer, *op. cit.*

18. Elshtain, *op. cit.* p. 3.

19. Christiansen and Powers extend the section of the Just War theory concerning blockades and sieges to sanctions and conclude that a comparison is not self-evident. After considering the Just War Doctrine as a whole, I argue that – with some modifications to the terminology and the opportunities for application – the doctrine does indeed offer insights for evaluating the imposition of and continuation of sanctions, in part by the distinction between *jus ad* and *jus in*. An important but controversial assumption, however, is that in some respects free trade is analogous to peace, as sanctions are to war. See Christiansen and Powers, *op. cit.*, pp. 97-120.

20. Self-interest is a factor here: the individual EU member-states need stable neighbours. Democracies can be held to agreements more easily than unpredictable totalitarian regimes. The United States, on the other hand, can easily dominate undemocratic Mexico and therefore sees less benefit in conditions that it considers 'soft'. See the European Council resolution of 28 November 1991 in Christiane Duparc (1993). *The European Community and Human Rights*. Luxembourg: Office for Official Publications of the European Communities; Daniela Napoli, 'The European Union's Foreign Policy and Human Rights', in Nanette A. Neuwahl and Allan Rosas, Eds. (1995). *The European Union and Human Rights*. The Hague: Kluwer Law International, pp. 297-312.

21. Even in these cases, each situation will need to be examined separately to determine whether it has become unacceptable, and whether trade should be suspended or continued.

22. For this statement's empirical foundations, see Hazelzet, *op. cit.*, pp. 34-61. Here, the US and the EU take contrasting approaches in their respective uses of trade measures to promote democratization. Cuba is the most illustrative example: the EU subjects trade to conditions but provides aid to facilitate satisfying these conditions; the United States continues to isolate Cuba without having brought the country any closer to democracy in the past 45 years. Only very recently have the Americans changed their approach. In January 1996 Clinton, following heavy international pressure, suspended the Helms/Burton Act once again, 'claiming that the allies informed him they would try to promote the introduction of democracy in Cuba.' (*NRC Handelsblad*, 4 January 1996, p. 13.)

23. The principles of the Just War Doctrine are listed in: Elshtain, *op. cit.*, pp. 98-103; Holmes, *op. cit.*, p. 164. For the arguments supporting and the specific adaptation of the Just War principles to achieve a Just Trade Doctrine, see Hazelzet (1996), *op. cit.*, pp. 24-33.

24. This criterion means that the arguments of both parties in the conflict are acknowledged as legitimate and just. Both parties should therefore recognize the limits of their 'just cause' and pursue their goals with commensurate restraint (see Elshtain, *op. cit.*, pp. 98-103).

25. A convincing ethical argument cannot be summed up in a few paragraphs. For a detailed application to empirical material, see Hazelzet, *op. cit.*, pp. 34-57. In

my dissertation I examined the following cases according to the Just Sanctions Doctrine: China, Colombia and the association treaties of the EU ('conditioned trade in order to promote good'); Haiti, Nigeria and Cuba ('sanctioned trade in order to prevent harm'); Iraq and Serbia-Montenegro ('no trade in order to punish evil').

26. While this case study is written in the past tense, the situation exists to this day.
27. Since the sanctions coincided with military force, the effects of the two measures are difficult to distinguish in some cases.
28. Nincic and Wallensteen, *op. cit.*, p. 6.
29. At one point, Iraqis who had fled in fear of their lives could request political asylum in various countries.
30. *The New York Times*, 22 May 1996. A study by the Harvard School of Public Health found 'strong evidence that the Gulf War and trade sanctions caused a threefold increase in mortality among Iraqi children under five years of age'. Quoted from: Patrick Clawson, 'Sanctions as Punishment, Enforcement, and Prelude to Further Action', in *Ethics and International Affairs*, Vol. 7 (1993), pp. 17-37. Although the share of blame resulting from the destruction of the war and the civil unrest is unclear, the countries imposing sanctions cannot escape their responsibility. See also the report by the Center for Economic and Social Rights (CESR), 1996. *UN Sanctions Suffering: A Human Rights Assessment of United Nations Sanctions on Iraq.* The arguments in the report include the assertion that the 'oil for food' agreement was far from sufficient to supply the population with food and medical care. See also: James C. Ngobi.,'The United Nations Experience with Sanctions', in Cortright and Lopez, Eds., *op. cit.*, pp. 17-29.
31. This is one of Michael Walzer's great insights, *op. cit.*
32. Noam J. Zohar, 'Boycott, Crime, and Sin: Ethical and Talmudic Responses to Injustice Abroad', in *Ethics and International Affairs*, Vol. 7 (1993), pp. 39-53.
33. On Haiti, see Claudette A. Werleigh, 'The Use of Sanctions in Haiti: Assessing the Economic Realities', in Cortright and Lopez, *op. cit.*, pp. 161-172. On Serbia, see Christiansen and Powers, *op. cit.*, p. 106.
34. Henk van Luijk (1993). *Om redelijk gewin. Oefeningen in bedrijfsethiek.* Amsterdam: Boom, p. 146.
35. C.A.J. Herkströter, *NRC Handelsblad,* 12 October 1996.

Winde Evenhuis

Martha Meijer worked for the Dutch section of Amnesty International from 1977 to 1994, first as the country coordinator for Indonesia and from 1988 as a board member and chairwoman. From 1992 to 1994, Meijer coordinated the Indonesian Documentation and Information Centre (INDOC). In 1994 she became the director of the Netherlands Humanist Committee on Human Rights (HOM) in Utrecht. In 1998 she also chaired the Dutch national platform commemorating the fiftieth anniversary of the UDHR and serves on the Dutch Human Rights Forum (*Breed Mensenrechten Overleg*). Meijer is a consultant, advisor, trainer and evaluator for human rights projects all over the world. In 1996 and 1999 she was an observer at the elections in Bosnia-Herzegovina and Indonesia.

8

THE HUMAN DIMENSION

Human Rights Impact Assessment as an Instrument

Martha Meijer

> *The supreme consideration is man.*
> Mahatma Gandhi

This contribution is intended as an effort to devise a human rights impact assessment as a foreign policy instrument. A human rights impact assessment entails analyzing foreign policy consequences and evaluating possible contributions to respect for human rights. Ideally, such an impact assessment is both reactive (which interventions yielded which results?) and proactive (which policy is indicated in which situation?). The English term used by Amnesty International reveals clearly that the idea of a human rights impact assessment is derived from the idea of an environmental impact assessment. Such an analysis considers several factors and examines how a given situation may affect human rights conditions.

The assumption that associating human rights conditions with international relations (conditionality) is morally acceptable figures in the debate about a human rights impact assessment. Presuming that human rights are universally applicable implicitly entails international responsibility for promoting respect for human rights all over the world, in part through one's own foreign policy. The need for corresponding priorities and choices is obvious but has not been argued in public until recently.

This contribution aims to stimulate the debate by examining the elements that a human rights impact assessment might comprise and trying to situate them in the overall context. The intention is not to achieve the final result but to encourage a more extensive substantive debate.

After substantiating the need for a human rights impact assessment, I will outline the current policy framework that determines the context of the human rights impact assessment. The following steps in the assessment process are then elaborated and several factors and strategies mentioned that affect the policy's evaluation. Next, the theoretical image is illustrated by applying it to an imaginary country (Nutopia). The contribution ends with several conclusions and recommendations.

The Desirability of a Human Rights Impact Assessment

Thus far, an explicit mechanism for assessing the impact of interventions on foreign policy has been difficult to realize. The different parties in foreign policy – governments, non-governmental organizations (NGOs), development partners, trade partners – are unable to agree on whether conditionality (i.e. associating human rights with other international relations) is acceptable. Nor have they reached common ground regarding the value of applying general strategies and criteria in specific situations. A human rights impact assessment facilitates discussion of conditionality's intrinsic moral acceptability. Several criteria make conditionality itself openly assessable.

Human rights have always been a trading commodity, long before the conception of conditionality. For centuries, countries have been pressured to improve respect for human rights. One example concerns the Peace of Westphalia in 1648, where freedom of religion was negotiated and treatment of minorities guaranteed.

Such negotiations have also involved underlying interests other than respect for human rights. All too often, self-interest, economic interests, protection of sympathetic movements or coalition interests are factors in a government's condemnation of human rights violations. Accordingly, objective standards benefit everybody.

States are accountable to each other about their human rights situation.[1] This observation arises from the transnational relevance of human rights (in both legal and moral respects) and from carefully considered self-interest. States also have an obligation to hold each other responsible for the conduct of others and to associate sanctions with this obligation through foreign policy interventions. In the Dutch constitution this obligation is stipulated in Article 90: 'The government shall promote development of the international legal order.'

Imposing sanctions on human rights situations elsewhere can obviously take several forms in international transactions (e.g. encouraging positive changes and blocking negative ones, imposing conditions or sanctions). Such interventions need to be accounted for, however, both in one's country and with respect to the state concerned (i.e. affected) and the other states subject to such a policy. In this accountability procedure, objective standards are important for reaching conclusions, elaborating standards and setting precedents.

Moreover devising a human rights impact assessment enables a government to balance various subordinate interests that figure in international relations. Deciphering interests, objectives, possible consequences and strategies will help formulate a more balanced impression than using implicit associations, presumptions and argumentation.

Several other myths have arisen regarding the importance of human rights in formulating policy. Some believe that a country's human rights situation will improve if economic ties exist with other countries. Others believe that international contact reinforces a dictatorial regime's power. Both arguments apply only in part or selectively. Making interests explicit assesses the value of such implicit assumptions and renders them verifiable. Each case is different and will be judged on its own merits, and a human rights impact assessment is appropriate for this purpose. The impact assessment is not, however, a manual with the magic answer.

Terminology

In arguments concerning a human rights impact assessment, devising clear definitions and straightforward terminology is important for all international transactions. Although differences and similarities are inherent in all situations, straightforward wording certainly complicates arbitrary interventions and a secret agenda and averts political demagogy.

States establish, break off or change international relations based on various and, in some cases, confidential assessments. The interventions may be confidential as well. On the other hand, human rights issues – which concern the relationship between the state and the citizen – may also be evaluated by the government's counterpart: the parliament and NGOs as representatives of the individual citizens. Governments should account for their human rights policy to the best of their ability and in unambiguous terms, with due regard for any confidentiality.

Conditionality is defined here as the instrument with which one government pressures another one to improve human rights policy and practice by imposing conditions on the international relations (whether bilateral or multilateral) between the countries concerned. Such pressure may take the form of mild encouragement or reinforcement of current – positive – trends or may consist of silent diplomacy to prevent human rights violations. The carrot and the stick approach is another option, combining efforts to reason with threats of more severe measures. The most extreme forms of pressure are suspension of diplomatic relations, imposition of an embargo or open condemnation in the multilateral UN context of the Human Rights Commission or the Security Council.

International relations are relations between governments of different states, between units within those states (e.g. trade partners) or between counterparts in different countries in a partnership agreement (e.g. with international development cooperation). With conditionality, all these relations are linked to human rights aspects. From this perspective, therefore, trade relations between the Netherlands and Germany are just as eligible for the human rights impact assessment as the development relationship between the Netherlands and Nigeria. Reciprocal interventions therefore merit consideration as well.

Involving all these relations in respect of human rights is not yet common practice. Power relationships greatly influence one government's sensitivity toward another government's measures. Moreover, power differences affect opportunities for setting conditions.

Nonetheless, we need to examine in the future whether imposing sanctions on trade and other relations in these cases as well is desirable and politically feasible, for example if the Dutch government condemns the human rights policy of a close ally.

The terms of positive and negative measures require a precise definition. In accordance with the Resolution of the Council and of the Member States meeting in the Council on Human Rights and Development of 1991[2], and Report No. 12 from the Advisory Committee on Human Rights in Foreign Policy (Adviescommissie Mensenrechten, ACM)[3], such measures include all interventions committed out of concern for human rights. Positive measures are intended to benefit the application of human rights. Negative ones involve restricting a relationship based on human rights considerations. Thus, positive and negative measures need not be diametrical opposites.

Although the ACM report concerns international economic relations such as international cooperation, trade in arms and other items and investments, these definitions are equally applicable in diplomatic and other negotiation situations. In diplomatic negotiations, negative measures often send a message of which the effectiveness may not be immediately quantifiable but can be analyzed empirically. Others have already discussed this subject in detail;[4] the results of such research would be useful in applying a human rights impact assessment.

Policy Framework

This section reviews policy documents such as acts, instructions, resolutions and memoranda determining the Dutch framework for the link between human rights and international relations. It also addresses the European Council Resolution and new Belgian legislation in this field (1994).

Human Rights in Foreign Policy

The important policy document *De rechten van de mens in buitenlands beleid* (Human rights in foreign policy) (1979), which remains a source of reference, defines the context of Dutch government policy on human rights. It establishes that human rights are a cornerstone in foreign policy and submits that the government shall act against gross and ongoing human rights violations, provided other interests do not suffer unacceptable damage in the process. It lists possible actions, ranging from silent diplomacy to public condemnation. In between lies a broad spectrum of interventions to be used effectively. The document does not specify ways to select means and evaluate effectiveness.

The document obliges the government to submit five-year policy implementation reports to the Lower House. These progress reports (1987, 1991, 1997), however, provide only a cursory analysis of actions taken. Successive governments have maintained that keeping interventions confidential will make future actions more effective. Reports may therefore be harmful by their very nature. Nonetheless, the progress reports show that the document continues to define general policy and does so broadly enough for ongoing public and political debates to address the practical significance of the term 'cornerstone'. In considering whether to discontinue or suspend development cooperation, as with Indonesia and Surinam, the other interests ('cornerstones' as well) and political assessments that often went unpublicized were decisive. Public debate on these decisions is all but impossible, and accusations of inconsistent policy are imminent.

According to the document, development cooperation policy is contingent upon human rights conditions. The very restriction of conditions to countries to which the Netherlands provides such aid turns this pressure – in the view of the government and people in that country – into the imposition of views based on a position of superiority, namely that of the donor country against the developing country.

One reservation is in order here. Development theories attribute progressively less value to the term developing country. The recipient country is no longer unilaterally dependent on the country giving the aid. The donor has an interest in good development in the recipient country, even regarding respect for human rights. Moreover, the donor derives great economic benefit from its role as a donor through more intensive relations. The recipient country can therefore exercise its power with respect to the donor as well. Indonesia's suspension in 1992 of its development cooperation relationship with the Netherlands illustrates this situation.

Another argument against restricting conditionality to development cooperation relationships is that human rights violations are by no means exclusive to developing countries. The obligation to intervene in the event of human rights violations in neighbouring countries, fellow EU member-states or allies is as great as with human rights violations elsewhere. The severity of the human rights violations should be the decisive factor. Moreover, policy would be more consistent and thus more convincing, if conditionality also prevailed among Western countries as a way of improving human rights situations.

The ACM Report

Although the ACM report *De rechten van de mens en internationale betrekkingen* (Human rights and international relations) focuses on the relationship between human rights and economic relations between states[5,] it addresses a few aspects of the conditionality debate as well. The ACM submits, for example, that affluence (the implementation of social-economic rights) is 'neither a condition nor a guarantee that these [civil and political] rights will be respected.' Nonetheless, constitutional states require a certain measure of economic development to function properly. The ACM also mentions the distribution of affluence. Conversely, 'successful and sustained economic and social development has consistently proved impossible in a repressive society.'[6]

The memorandum offers a variegated, albeit by now dated, impression of potential positive and negative measures in international economic relations. Since 1991 images of the world have changed dramatically, although the debate on broader acceptance of labour standards and a code of conduct for trans-border investments remains current. The report refers to the conventions of the International Labour Organization (ILO) and to the EC code of conduct concerning South Africa from 1977. It obviously does not mention the World Trade Organization (WTO), which was established only in 1995. The highlights of these debates, however, are starting to play a role in the WTO.

The report uses the concepts of positive and negative measures as indicated above. Positive measures promote respect for human rights in another country through education, support for civil society, independent media and the like. Measuring their effect is a fairly straightforward process.

Regarding the application of negative measures, the ACM identifies several possible objectives of such measures:

- as pressure tactics;
- as penal measures;
- to prevent violations;
- to avert involvement.

These objectives (intended effects) will not always coincide with a negative measure's effects; the areas of friction between the intended and the actual effects are especially important in conducting analysis for future interventions.

Redefinition of Foreign Policy

The cabinet comprising social democrats and liberals (1994) was unable to agree on the budgets for Foreign Affairs, Development Cooperation and Defence. The 'foreign triad' was redefined to bring about a joint, direct (i.e. without mediating steps involving these three ministries) policy on substantive, organizational and financial aspects. The resulting memorandum *De herijking van het buitenlands beleid* (Redefining of foreign policy) addresses both the policy's organizational aspects and changes in international and political contexts.[7]

The memorandum devotes little attention to the role of human rights in the redefined foreign policy. This oversight has been criticized extensively, including the remarks from several Dutch human rights organizations associated in the *Breed Mensenrechten Overleg (BMO)* (Dutch Human Rights Forum).[8] While the memorandum was being debated in the Lower House, some hard stands emerged on the role of human rights policy in foreign policy overall. This led to an organizational adjustment consisting of the establishment of a directorate for Human Rights, Good Governance and Democratization in the department.

European Council Resolution

This European Council Resolution of November 1991[9] is based on a resolution of 29 June 1991 which stated 'that respect for human rights, the rule of law and the existence of political institutions which are effective, accountable and enjoy democratic legitimacy are the basis for equitable development.' The resolution is also based on the statement of 21 July 1986 by the ministers of Foreign Affairs of the European Community, which reiterated that respect for, promotion of and guarantees concerning human rights were essential in international relations and were a cornerstone of European cooperation and of the relations between European member-states and third states.

After establishing that the member-states require a joint and consistent human rights policy, the resolution of November 1991 formulates several concrete guidelines, procedures and opportunities for action, which comprise both positive and negative measures.

The positive measures include:

- promoting respect for human rights in countries in transition toward greater democracy;
- supporting the organization of democratic elections, establishing democratic institutions and strengthening the constitutional state;
- improving the justice system, crime prevention and treatment of offenders;
- promoting the role of NGOs and other institutions contributing to a pluralist society;
- supporting efforts to ensure equal opportunities for all.

The importance of good governance is emphasized as well and is described in the resolution as follows:

- reasonable economic and social policy;
- democratic decision-making;
- sufficiently transparent style of government and financial accounting;
- a market-friendly, development-oriented environment;
- counter-corruption efforts;
- respect for the constitutional state, human rights and freedom of expression and of the press.

The resolution states that in the event of human rights violations or interruption of democratic processes, the EC and the member-states shall consider responding according to objective and equitable criteria. These criteria, however, remain unspecified. The resolution does indicate that the population should not suffer from actions taken by the government, and that in some cases intergovernmental aid can therefore be transferred to non-government channels. Humanitarian and emergency aid will continue in all cases.

This resolution has led to the publication of annual reports on the actions taken in this respect. These reports raise more questions than they answer. The 1994 report describes the EU/EC response to the bloodbath in Rwanda.[10] On 21 April 1994 the European Parliament condemned the fighting, mass murders and assassinations of the president and the prime minister. Horrified at the genocide, the Council of Ministers and the Commission discontinued all aid.

The 1995 report[11] notes, however, that development aid was suspended in April 1995 but restored following the signature of an agreement between the EU and the president of Rwanda on 8 July 1995. How consistent was this policy? In 1994 the aid was discontinued, while humanitarian and emergency aid should have continued under the 1991 agreements. Were NGOs given the opportunity to keep doing their work? In 1995 the aid was suspended: had it been restored after the genocide in 1994 and on what grounds? What guarantees did the new president of Rwanda give that led the aid to be resumed?

Still, these reports reflect *ad hoc* measures embodying a clear human rights mission: 'In December 1995 the ambassadors of the Troika of the EU[12] took steps concerning the foreign affairs of Zaire so that it would take measures with the aim of stopping the radio transmitter "Radio of Hate" from broadcasting from Zaire.' [13] The measures and the related reports, however, are far from consistent.

Belgian Legislation

The Belgian legislation of 1994[14] requires that the Belgian government submit a written report to the House and the Senate each year before 31 March addressing the status of generally accepted human rights in every country with which Belgium has signed a general convention on development cooperation. The report must include the following sections:

a. A general sketch of the political and economic situation.

b. An overview of the human rights situation, especially the incidence of:

- political killings and lethal maltreatment;
- disappearances;
- torture and other cruel, inhuman and humiliating treatment or punishment;
- arbitrary detentions;
- denial of a fair trial;
- privacy violations.

c. The degree of respect for civil and political rights.

d. The degree of respect for social and economic rights.

e. The attitude of the local authorities toward international and non-governmental investigations of alleged human rights violations.

The principles underlying the Belgian legislation are derived from the EC resolution of 28 November 1991. This makes Belgium the only EU member-state known to have adopted the agreements in the EC resolution in its national legislation. The measures are elaborated in an explanatory memorandum as well. The positive measures are as follows:

- technical and logistic cooperation to improve the justice system;
- support from human rights organizations;
- legal and medical support for political prisoners and aid for their family members;
- financial aid for deliberations between government and opposition (whether violent or peaceful);
- training of policemen and other officials dealing with human rights and treatment of prisoners.

The restrictive measures (in ascending order of severity) include:

- diplomatic interventions (bilateral or multilateral);
- announcement of steps regarding the continuation of programmes;
- deferral of programme ratification;
- reallocation of funds to other operators, such as NGOs, or to other sectors, such as medical programmes;

- suspension of specific aid budgets, especially those that will have an immediate effect on responsible parties, such as balance-of-payments support.

The Human Rights Impact Assessment

Principles

In every human rights debate, discussions arise revealing the different premises of the participants that underlie the variety of opinions. Assumptions are inevitable but need to be made explicit. This section is based on the following principles:

a. Human rights are universal, indivisible and mutually dependent. This position, based on the Universal Declaration of Human Rights, was reaffirmed by all UN member-states during the UN Human Rights Conference in Vienna (1993).

b. States are accountable to one another regarding their human rights record. Conversely, states are entitled and obliged to hold each other accountable and to initiate improvement, even across national borders.

c. In interventions designed to improve respect for human rights, positive measures should be the first priority. They will improve a population's ability to defend its rights. If the positive measures are ineffective or insufficiently effective, negative measures are the next step.

d. Interventions intended to strengthen respect for human rights should include extensive consideration for civil society as an infrastructure for human rights (i.e. the channels where people operate to improve such respect). Leading agents in these channels include social organizations, independent courts and legal professionals, the media, education, people and organizations involved in social-economic rights and improvement of opportunities for personal enrichment.

Assessment

If the analogy with the original environmental impact assessment prevails, specific interventions are usually assessed without devising policy. This process leads to *ad hoc* measures and fails to do justice to cumulative factors from different interventions. For the sake of consistency, a human rights standard should apply in formulating and establishing policy.

The assessment process entails several steps arising in different stages of decision-making that continuously influence each other. In the first step regional policy documents are formulated reflecting the human rights situation by country. This leads to the second step, which involves formulating ways to improve the situation. These opportunities are then elaborated into interventions or projects and the expected human rights consequences analyzed. During implementation human rights aspects are taken into account again and more concretely. All these steps are anticipatory or proactive. After (or better yet, during) a project or intervention's implementation, an evaluation takes place (monitoring). The conclusions are applied at earlier stages in subsequent projects and interventions or in ones geared toward other countries. Table 1 depicts the process in a diagram.

Table 1. Assessment and policy development

Step in the process	Influences	Achieves the result
1. Description of the human rights situation	Policy document, criteria for projects and interventions	Focused projects and interventions are proposed
2. Advance formulation of projects and interventions: opportunities and obstacles	Proposals concerning the manner of execution of projects and interventions	The proposals address aspects that promote human rights
3. Realization of opportunities for promoting human rights	Execution of projects and interventions	Alternatives are evaluated according to their impact on human rights
4. Investigation of actual impact on human rights situation and interventions	Project evaluation	Conclusions are formulated for future policy and intended interventions

In testing and drafting policy a wide variety of factors and strategies are conceivable that will promote or curtail human rights. The ones indicated below illustrate the general idea. Ideas and debates about these factors are only beginning to crystallize. The following section is not intended to be comprehensive. Rather, it encourages an ongoing and never-ending debate. Strategies are dynamic by definition and cannot be captured for eternity.

Promoting Factors

Several social factors promote respect for human rights. Often, though not always, there is an inhibiting counterpart factor, as well as a sliding scale and mutual cohesion in most cases. The promoting factors include:

a. jurisprudence
b. civil society
c. economic development
d. independent media
e. education

a. *Jurisprudence*

Independent law enforcement is essential for the legal order. A population unable to obtain retribution via the courts will either give up or will resort to other, illegal tactics. As a consequence, the legal order will deteriorate. Law schools are therefore an important area of attention, as are additional refinements in this area. In allocating educational grants, programmes in criminal or constitutional law should receive preference over ones in notarial law. Law enforcement will also benefit from dedicated lawyers, free legal counsel, outspoken legal aid organizations, condemnation of police abuse and legal documentation centres.

b. *Civil Society*

A variegated social centre field will increase the likelihood that citizens will mount joint efforts, thereby finding strength in numbers, to demand justification of actions or seek recourse from their government. This will raise civic participation. Civil society (NGOs and civil initiatives) nearly always deserves support in human rights issues. In addition to human rights organizations, cases in point include women's organizations, religious congregations, environmental organizations or grassroots organizations, such as neighbourhood committees resisting speculative urban expansion or road building. These smaller targets for reinforcement are difficult to identify from abroad, although they often exist as umbrella movements, regional initiatives or facilitating and educational institutes.

A dilemma may arise with pseudo-NGOs in countries where NGOs are prohibited (in China they are known as GONGOs or governmental NGOs). Knowledge of the local situation is important here: in Indonesia the government has established a human rights commission that has increasingly come to resemble an independent NGO over the years. Another dilemma may arise if foreign support to an outspoken NGO is viewed as foreign interference, and thus makes the NGO a target of government pressure.

c. *Economic Development*

Another factor promoting human rights is the emergence of an affluent middle class, which will have higher expectations and a vested interest in its own material wealth on the one hand and will feel capable of defending its rights openly on the other hand. In some countries consumer organizations are powerful forces in civil society. This also reveals the argument about the emergence of civil society, as people will organize to achieve social goals only once they have some certainty about where their next meal will come from. Local unions are a special case: they raise political awareness among previously unorganized poor people. This ability gives unions unique opportunities for mobilizing widespread political support and may also cause rivalry between unions on the one hand and human rights or other political organizations (which often hail from the elite) on the other hand. Sometimes political organizations accuse unions of recruiting their members under false pretences – better working conditions for the poor – and of using their numbers as a weapon in the political struggle against an authoritarian government.

d. *Independent Media*

Reporting freedom is indispensable for involving people in what is happening in a country and in enabling them to form their own opinions.

Media credibility, insight into the government's operating mechanism and room for critical reflections inspire active expectations among readers or other consumers about ways to influence national or local administrations.

In countries that permit independent media, commercialism may lead to overly biased or apolitical reporting. In this sense the mergers between Western newspapers are cause for concern. From a human rights perspective, stronger anti-cartel legislation in the media and more rigid conditions for commercial television stations might bring improvement. International relations could address this issue as well.

e. *Education*

The availability of educational facilities depends on a country's macro-economic development, although opportunities for using these facilities depend on outside influences. Education is important for people to participate in the government of their city or country, from the very start of their schooling. Literacy greatly improves one's means for interacting with society. The more educated have higher expectations of their future and are more impatient; they are therefore more outspoken. Education is an important factor in the emergence of a vibrant civil society, a strong middle class and a public that is sufficiently well-rounded to appreciate independent media.

At the same time, however, certain educational structures can have a discriminatory effect. In such cases the above advantages are available to only a small group, which can become the accomplice of the ruling elite, just as corruption turns people into accomplices.

Inhibiting Factors

The following section addresses several factors that inhibit respect for or awareness of human rights. They are not always counterparts of promoting factors (independent media versus censorship) but are often essentially neutral factors that – considering their effect on human rights situations in some parts of the world – may lead to negative evaluations, such as culture and gender.[15] The factors are as follows:

a. corruption
b. historical ties
c. gender

d. culture

e. censorship

a. *Corruption*

The tentacles of corruption can penetrate all sectors of society. Corruption renders every obligation to answer for one's actions devoid of meaning, as everything is for sale. The examples include judges bribed by criminals and authorities alike, commission fees that must be kept secret and therefore force high-level accountants to lie, and land speculation at the expense of farmers. All these wrongs are impossible to reverse, because the courts are corrupt as well. Corruption abets corruption. Judges in a country where corruption is rampant are evaluated by the authorities according to their susceptibility to corruption. Honest judges are a burden and should be promoted out of their position or lured into a corruption scandal. Economists know they are looking for trouble if they investigate corruption's disastrous economic consequences and must therefore lie low. Investors pay a standard ten per cent commission, which they recover by paying low wages. This practice discourages them from allowing union activities.

b. *Historical Ties*

Historical ties will inevitably influence relations between two countries. Most situations concern a colonial past or one tainted by war. The effect is usually negative; relations are assessed on more than business grounds alone. The former Dutch colonies of Indonesia and Surinam are cases in point, while other West-European states face these irrationalities in their foreign policy as well (e.g. Germany and Croatia, France and Algeria, Belgium and the Congo).

This largely negative effect on relations is usually attributable to an unresolved past or an earlier trauma. Coming to terms with the situation often involves dredging up former human rights violations – by whichever side – that were not settled through a more or less objective trial. The underlying insurmountable obstacles cause ongoing frustration. (How can we judge past colonial abuses today? How can we find reliable material about a genocide? Who is accountable within the state apparatus?) While the historical past cannot be erased, we must accept it as a fact and consider it rationally in current relations.

c. *Gender*

The relationships, roles and mutual positions of men and women in a society greatly determine the realization of human rights (especially for women). In many cases cultural traditions exclude women from certain rights that pervade all walks of life. Violence against women is universal and inspires resistance and agitation in all countries. Many years of insufficient attention to women's rights legitimize the view that the subject merits greater consideration. Cultures and tradition requires a dialogue with and between women and men as well as initiation and reinforcement of efforts to raise awareness.

d. *Culture*

Whether as a general factor or in its local particularities, culture need not be an inhibiting factor as to respect for human rights. On the contrary, tolerant cultures, by virtue of their openness, promote a natural sensitivity toward the rights of others and those of other groups. Some groups, however, use culture to draw attention to themselves at another group's expense and are therefore often intolerant toward others. Often culture also serves to maintain an elite's position of power within a cultural group.

e. *Censorship*

Censorship is an infectious disease. The indirect, intimidating effect of censorship on the press usually outweighs the immediate effect of a prohibition of publication. Banning a newspaper inspires fear and restraint among other media. Many editorial boards of newspapers in countries with censorship have a commission for self-censorship that evaluates whether articles and cartoons on sensitive subjects are admissible. Cartoons are often a final resort for expressing verbal and non-verbal criticism. Supporting a courageous, independent source of information thus has a greater impact on human rights situations than circulation figures reveal. People glimpse a shred of integrity and become bolder as a result.

In addition to analyzing a country's actual situation, the human rights impact assessment involves devising a strategy for improvement. The above factors need to be examined and alternative measures considered and their effectiveness evaluated. The aforementioned principle of priority for positive measures requires immense creativity, as well as a particularly stringent impact assessment, before resorting to negative measures. Finally, combining positive and negative measures may bring about a focused strategy.

Positive Measures

In its resolution of November 1991 the European Council of Ministers formulated the following positive measures for certain situations:

- promoting respect for human rights in countries in transition toward greater democracy;
- supporting democratic elections, setting up democratic institutions and strengthening the constitutional state;
- reinforcing the justice system, crime prevention and offender treatment;
- promoting the role of NGOs and other institutions that contribute to a pluralist society;
- supporting efforts to provide equal opportunities for all.

The considerations associated with the aforementioned factors easily bring to mind measures indicated in certain situations (identified through the actual analysis). Such measures include supporting independent unions and a free press, fighting corruption and educating women and poor people. Facts about the local situation in a country need to be gathered and opportunities identified. In reaching new trade agreements we can examine which sectors of trade are free of corruption and focus on these areas. In the event of a smooth diplomatic relationship of trust with a country, we can explore opportunities for forming a coalition that might benefit multilateral respect for human rights.

Negative Measures

The European resolution lists a number of possible negative measures but stops short of indicating the criteria to be applied: 'guided by objective and equitable criteria.' Clearly, however, the response 'will avoid penalising the population for governmental actions,' and the preferred form or channel will leave society's poorest unaffected or will affect them as little as possible. In all cases humanitarian and emergency aid shall be continued according to the resolution.

Several observations come to mind. The absence of fixed criteria will lead the EU to impose a negative measure on member-states for different reasons in each case. Aggressive policy becomes mired in a tiresome struggle involving endless negotiations and false redmption. First the EU member-states will need to formulate clear criteria together and agree on decision-making procedures.

The negative measures are also too vague and optional. Belgian legislation is far more thorough in this respect and lists all possible steps (see above). Here, too, the intended impact escapes the picture and is therefore not assessed according to its effectiveness either.

Often a multilateral measure will clearly have a greater impact but will be harder to achieve as well. In recent years the European Union has come to resemble a giant with feet of clay: a large, unwieldy body that appeals to national governments as a subterfuge. The ACM report describing the different functions of negative measures provides useful input for the effectiveness debate:

- as a pressure tactic;
- as a form of punishment;
- to prevent violations from being committed;
- to avoid involvement in perpetuating the regime.

Analyzing more of such functions and objectives enables strategies to be formulated for a more consistent policy.

Nutopia

The following illustration of the emergence of the assessment process is based on the imaginary country of Nutopia. This sketch is obviously one-dimensional and merely serves to depict the ideas behind the human rights impact assessment and to stimulate discussion.

Initial Situation

The imaginary state of Nutopia has friendly diplomatic and economic relations and good development cooperation and cultural connections with the Netherlands. Nutopia has no historical ties with the

Netherlands. The country suffers from rampant corruption. The most common human rights violations include maltreatment during detention, unfair trials and discrimination against a minority.

The first step is to describe and analyze the human rights situation in Nutopia. Various sources of information are used, including special reports from the embassy, UN special rapporteurs and human rights organizations. Information from local organizations indicates whether or not they are independent. An overview relates the existing legislation, the practices and demonstrable violations, and reveals whether or not they are ongoing. Both civil and political and social-economic rights are addressed, albeit so globally that the overview enables policy formulation.[16] This description is also associated with the political and social-economic relations in Nutopia.

The policy documents offer a global outline of foreign policy on Nutopia: diplomatic and economic interests, cultural priorities and the opportunities for development cooperation. They also review the human rights situation and indicate which human rights violations need to be dealt with first or most dramatically.

Formulating Opportunities and Obstacles

Establishing the general policy is followed by an examination of the potential impact of interventions and projects on the human rights situation. Opportunities and obstacles regarding promotion of respect for human rights in Nutopia are formulated as well.

Suppose Nutopia's special opportunities are the fact that English is the official language, the relationship of diplomacy and trust that the Netherlands has established in the recent past and vast coffee exports to the Netherlands. The obstacles include corruption and the hostility between Nutopia and its neighbour. The minority that suffers discrimination pertains to the same ethnic group as the majority of the population in the neighbouring country.

All things considered, the opportunities lie in education (since English is used for general communication) and in the reciprocal interests resulting from coffee exports. Promoting permanent respect for human rights, however, requires eliminating obstacles such as tense diplomatic relations with neighbouring countries and corruption.

Concretization: Proposals for Projects and Interventions

In this stage, proposals arising from the aforementioned opportunities and obstacles are made concrete, along with their potential influence on the human rights situation and the intended effects.

Suppose a group of independent law enforcement officials with integrity protects the interests of the citizens in Nutopia. Domestically, they will have difficulty prevailing because they will be targets of unprovable accusations of corruption. The Netherlands supports this group's independence by proposing an initiative to provide legal professionals with additional training through a development cooperation project, which serves to enable this group to pass its ideas on to the younger generation.

In Nutopia another movement against corruption is trying to form a coalition with a similar movement in the neighbouring country. The governments, however, want to keep the borders closed to prevent the anti-corruption movements from becoming well established. The Netherlands engages in diplomatic mediation between both countries with two objectives in mind: reducing unrest in the region and creating opportunities for social organizations (including the anti-corruption movement) to work together across the border. Whether such cooperation will exacerbate ethnic tension is unclear. Coalitions may emerge along ethnic lines.

Nutopia has only one radio station. The station is run by the Mafia, which controls part of the coffee trade as well. The radio station provides information reflecting a strong ethnic bias and increasing the likelihood of an internal conflict. In its economic policy, the Netherlands has convinced Dutch coffee importers not to purchase from this Mafia, thereby reducing the funds available to the Radio of Hate transmitter. In addition, the Netherlands supports other, more objective news media through its cultural programme.

Evaluation

Throughout and after their implementation, projects and interventions require continuous monitoring to determine their actual impact. In the examples listed above, the method of achieving the desired effect needs to be established. Perhaps the special programme for law students is subject to such severe government disapproval that students are afraid to register. Perhaps the programme might be stationed elsewhere and opened to law students from different countries. Such action would promote mutual exchange between participants. Perhaps the proposed effort to negotiate will arouse so much suspicion that it will need to be abandoned after a tentative start. In this case, encouraging a regional umbrella organization might be wiser. The ban on the coffee trade could lead the Netherlands to be prosecuted by the WTO at the initiative of the Nutopian government, which the Mafia has apparently penetrated as well.

These and other dilemmas will recur constantly and will affect human rights policy. New strategies will be necessary to achieve results in the long run. In this dynamic plan the final evaluations will generate new impulses for subsequent choices, and comparisons of interventions in different countries may yield new insights. The human rights impact assessment is not a panacea for all human rights problems. The more it is elaborated, however, and the more experiences are included, the greater will be the insight into the possible consequences of certain interventions. This will lead to a better human rights policy and will ensure clearer and more concise feedback, assessment and final accountability.

Conclusions and Recommendations

A policy on conditionality – setting conditions in foreign policy based on another country's human rights situation – must by definition be morally justifiable and consistent. Analyzing the situation and the opportunities for improvement may lead to a strategy. This policy should be subject to a democratic decision-making process through public and political debate. As a result, human rights policy will become assessable. The preceding paragraphs present arguments supporting conditionality and a human rights impact assessment as an instrument to this end.

Accountability is necessary in both domestic public and political opinion and in international politics. The human rights impact assessment should be one of the international instruments for states to monitor each other and coordinate policy.

While many will find such a recommendation unrealistic at this time, concrete opportunities for compiling factual reports in various 'foreign countries' are being considered. Each year, the United States – the world's self-appointed but not officially recognized policeman – compiles an overview of the human rights situation in nearly all countries in the world. This annual publication of over a thousand pages, the *Country Report on Human Rights Practices*, is drafted by the US State Department. This authorship colours the information. Anybody with some knowledge of countries who examines the work will notice the omissions or exaggerations intended to promote the US government. The facts are distorted based on an implicit, pre-selected political strategy.

Alternatively, an independent institute might compile the actual overview. The department and the institute (as an advisory organ) could discuss the possible policy consequences. In the end those with political responsibility make policy decisions and submit them to the Congress.

Thus far, the Dutch Foreign Office has drafted regional policy plans. They are very broad and have recently begun to be elaborated country by country by the embassies. The role of human rights considerations is difficult to determine, since these country documents are not public. Any incidents that arise are subsequently discussed *ad hoc*. There is no element of consistency, neither by country nor by period.

While general acceptance of such a human rights impact assessment in foreign policy will take years to develop, the similar sentiment elicited by an environmental effect analysis two decades ago offers a glimmer of hope. The above conveys only a general impression of what will be necessary in the future, given the increasingly cross-border nature of human rights. Universality is the foundation for states to hold each other to international agreements. At present they lack the right instruments. The human rights impact assessment might be one such device. Human rights organizations will need to initiate debate on the consistency of their government's human rights policy and to stimulate it with their ideas about criteria, factors and strategies.

In this discussion on abstract policy, criteria and strategy determination, we lose sight of the essential dimension depicted by Mahatma Gandhi in his statement included as this contribution's motto:

'the supreme consideration is man.' Assessing whether the policy complies with this consideration specifically requires input from people who evaluate measures according to the human dimension. This also explains the value of the ANC recommendation (before apartheid was abolished) that South Africa be completely isolated by the international community. The people concerned made this choice on their own. In politics, such grassroots considerations are necessary to make the right decision. People and human rights organizations are indispensable in this decision-making process, and the human rights impact assessment serves as an instrument here. Only then will a politically consistent and assessable human rights policy become possible.

NOTES

1. Menno Tjeerd Kamminga (1990). *Inter-State Accountability for Violations of Human Rights.* Dissertation. Leiden: University of Leiden.
2. Council of the European Community. *Resolution of the Council and of the Member States Meeting in the Council on Human Rights, Democracy and Development,* 1538th Council Meeting Development Co-operation, Brussels, 28 November 1991, 9555/91 (Presse 217-G).
3. Advisory Committee on Human Rights and Foreign Policy (ACM). *De rechten van de mens en de internationale economische betrekkingen,* (Report No. 12), The Hague, 29 May 1991. ACM, PO Box 20061, 2500 EB The Hague.
4. See Peter Baehr *et al.* Eds. (1995). *Human Rights in Developing Countries: Yearbook 1995.* The Hague: Kluwer Law International.
5. ACM Report No. 12, *op. cit.*
6. *Ibid.,* p. 74.
7. Ministry of Foreign Affairs. *De herijking van het buitenlands beleid.* (Dutch Government Proposal Redefining Foreign Policy). The Hague, September 1995.
8. Comment of the Dutch Human Rights Forum (BMO) on the Dutch government proposal Redefining Foreign Policy, October 1995.
9. *Ibid.,* Note 2.
10. European Commission, Directorate General for Development. *Report on the Implementation in 1994 of the Resolution of the Council and the Member States Meeting in the Council on Human Rights, Democracy and Development, Adopted on 28 November 1991.* Brussels: VIII/1406/95-EN, p. 16.
11. European Commission, Directorate General for Development. *Report on the Implementation in 1995 of the Resolution of the Council and the Member States Meeting in the Council on Human Rights, Democracy and Development, Adopted on 28 November 1991.* Brussels: VIII/4, p. 21.
12. The presidency of the European Union rotates every six months among the fifteen member-states. The Troika is a forum comprising the three states of the

current, the former and the upcoming presidency.

13. European Commission, *op.cit.*, Note 11, p. 22.

14. Act to verify the policy on development cooperation as to its compliance with respect for human rights; approved by the House on 19 May 1993, and by the Senate on 20 January 1994, affirmed by His Majesty the King on 7 February 1994; *Belgisch Staatsblad*, N.94-2299, 13 September 1994.

15. Gender concerns the relationships, roles and positions between men and women in a society.

16. A brief checklist appears in the Belgian act on conditionality, *op. cit.*, Note 14. A detailed outline has been published in Baehr *et al.*, *op. cit.*, pp. 407-413.

Appendix

Universal Declaration of Human Rights

Adopted and proclaimed by General Assembly resolution 217 A (III) of 10 December 1948.

PREAMBLE

Whereas recognition of the inherent dignity and of the equal and inalienable rights of all members of the human family is the foundation of freedom, justice and peace in the world,

Whereas disregard and contempt for human rights have resulted in barbarous acts which have outraged the conscience of mankind, and the advent of a world in which human beings shall enjoy freedom of speech and belief and freedom from fear and want has been proclaimed as the highest aspiration of the common people,

Whereas it is essential, if man is not to be compelled to have recourse, as a last resort, to rebellion against tyranny and oppression, that human rights should be protected by the rule of law,

Whereas it is essential to promote the development of friendly relations between nations,

Whereas the peoples of the United Nations have in the Charter reaffirmed their faith in fundamental human rights, in the dignity and worth of the human person and in the equal rights of men and women and have determined to promote social progress and better standards of life in larger freedom,

Whereas Member States have pledged themselves to achieve, in co-operation with the United Nations, the promotion of universal respect for and observance of human rights and fundamental freedoms,

Whereas a common understanding of these rights and freedoms is of the greatest importance for the full realization of this pledge,

Now, therefore the General Assembly proclaims this Universal Declaration of Human Rights as a common standard of achievement for all peoples and all nations, to the end that every individual and every organ of society, keeping this Declaration constantly in mind, shall strive by teaching and education to promote respect for these rights and freedoms and by progressive measures, national and international, to secure their universal and effective recognition and observance, both among the peoples of Member States themselves and among the peoples of territories under their jurisdiction.

Article 1
All human beings are born free and equal in dignity and rights. They are endowed with reason and conscience and should act towards one another in a spirit of brotherhood.

Article 2
Everyone is entitled to all the rights and freedoms set forth in this Declaration, without distinction of any kind, such as race, colour, sex, language, religion, political or other opinion, national or social origin, property, birth or other status. Furthermore, no distinction shall be made on the basis of the political, jurisdictional or international status of the country or territory to which a person belongs, whether it be independent, trust, non-self-governing or under any other limitation of sovereignty.

Article 3
Everyone has the right to life, liberty and security of person.

Article 4

No one shall be held in slavery or servitude; slavery and the slave trade shall be prohibited in all their forms.

Article 5

No one shall be subjected to torture or to cruel, inhuman or degrading treatment or punishment.

Article 6

Everyone has the right to recognition everywhere as a person before the law.

Article 7

All are equal before the law and are entitled without any discrimination to equal protection of the law. All are entitled to equal protection against any discrimination in violation of this Declaration and against any incitement to such discrimination.

Article 8

Everyone has the right to an effective remedy by the competent national tribunals for acts violating the fundamental rights granted him by the constitution or by law.

Article 9

No one shall be subjected to arbitrary arrest, detention or exile.

Article 10

Everyone is entitled in full equality to a fair and public hearing by an independent and impartial tribunal, in the determination of his rights and obligations and of any criminal charge against him.

Article 11

1) Everyone charged with a penal offence has the right to be presumed innocent until proved guilty according to law in a public trial at which he has had all the guarantees necessary for his defence.

2) No one shall be held guilty of any penal offence on account of any

act or omission which did not constitute a penal offence, under national or international law, at the time when it was committed. Nor shall a heavier penalty be imposed than the one that was applicable at the time the penal offence was committed.

Article 12

No one shall be subjected to arbitrary interference with his privacy, family, home or correspondence, nor to attacks upon his honour and reputation. Everyone has the right to the protection of the law against such interference or attacks.

Article 13

1) Everyone has the right to freedom of movement and residence within the borders of each State.

2) Everyone has the right to leave any country, including his own, and to return to his country.

Article 14

1) Everyone has the right to seek and to enjoy in other countries asylum from persecution.

2) This right may not be invoked in the case of prosecutions genuinely arising from non-political crimes or from acts contrary to the purposes and principles of the United Nations.

Article 15

1) Everyone has the right to a nationality.

2) No one shall be arbitrarily deprived of his nationality nor denied the right to change his nationality.

Article 16

1) Men and women of full age, without any limitation due to race, nationality or religion, have the right to marry and to found a family. They are entitled to equal rights as to marriage, during marriage and at its dissolution.

2) Marriage shall be entered into only with the free and full consent of the intending spouses.

3) The family is the natural and fundamental group unit of society and is entitled to protection by society and the State.

Article 17
1) Everyone has the right to own property alone as well as in association with others.
2) No one shall be arbitrarily deprived of his property.

Article 18
Everyone has the right to freedom of thought, conscience and religion; this right includes freedom to change his religion or belief, and freedom, either alone or in community with others and in public or private, to manifest his religion or belief in teaching, practice, worship and observance.

Article 19
Everyone has the right to freedom of opinion and expression; this right includes freedom to hold opinions without interference and to seek, receive and impart information and ideas through any media and regardless of frontiers.

Article 20
1) Everyone has the right to freedom of peaceful assembly and association.
2) No one may be compelled to belong to an association.

Article 21
1) Everyone has the right to take part in the government of his country, directly or through freely chosen representatives.
2) Everyone has the right of equal access to public service in his country.
3) The will of the people shall be the basis of the authority of government; this will shall be expressed in periodic and genuine elections which shall be by universal and equal suffrage and shall be held by secret vote or by equivalent free voting procedures.

Article 22

Everyone, as a member of society, has the right to social security and is entitled to realization, through national effort and international co-operation and in accordance with the organization and resources of each State, of the economic, social and cultural rights indispensable for his dignity and the free development of his personality.

Article 23

1) Everyone has the right to work, to free choice of employment, to just and favourable conditions of work and to protection against unemployment.

2) Everyone, without any discrimination, has the right to equal pay for equal work.

3) Everyone who works has the right to just and favourable remuneration ensuring for himself and his family an existence worthy of human dignity, and supplemented, if necessary, by other means of social protection.

4) Everyone has the right to form and to join trade unions for the protection of his interests.

Article 24

Everyone has the right to rest and leisure, including reasonable limitation of working hours and periodic holidays with pay.

Article 25

1) Everyone has the right to a standard of living adequate for the health and well-being of himself and of his family, including food, clothing, housing and medical care and necessary social services, and the right to security in the event of unemployment, sickness, disability, widowhood, old age or other lack of livelihood in circumstances beyond his control.

2) Motherhood and childhood are entitled to special care and assistance. All children, whether born in or out of wedlock, shall enjoy the same social protection.

Article 26

1) Everyone has the right to education. Education shall be free, at least

in the elementary and fundamental stages. Elementary education shall be compulsory. Technical and professional education shall be made generally available and higher education shall be equally accessible to all on the basis of merit.

2) Education shall be directed to the full development of the human personality and to the strengthening of respect for human rights and fundamental freedoms. It shall promote understanding, tolerance and friendship among all nations, racial or religious groups, and shall further the activities of the United Nations for the maintenance of peace.

3) Parents have a prior right to choose the kind of education that shall be given to their children.

Article 27

1) Everyone has the right freely to participate in the cultural life of the community, to enjoy the arts and to share in scientific advancement and its benefits.

2) Everyone has the right to the protection of the moral and material interests resulting from any scientific, literary or artistic production of which he is the author.

Article 28

Everyone is entitled to a social and international order in which the rights and freedoms set forth in this Declaration can be fully realized.

Article 29

1) Everyone has duties to the community in which alone the free and full development of his personality is possible.

2) In the exercise of his rights and freedoms, everyone shall be subject only to such limitations as are determined by law solely for the purpose of securing due recognition and respect for the rights and freedoms of others and of meeting the just requirements of morality, public order and the general welfare in a democratic society.

3) These rights and freedoms may in no case be exercised contrary to the purposes and principles of the United Nations.

Article 30

Nothing in this Declaration may be interpreted as implying for any State, group or person any right to engage in any activity or to perform any act aimed at the destruction of any of the rights and freedoms set forth herein.

BIBLIOGRAPHY

Abdullah, Taufik (1993), 'The Formation of a Political Tradition in the Malay World', in Anthony Reid, Ed. *The Making of Islamic Discourse in Southeast Asia.* (Monash Papers on Southeast Asia, No. 27). Melbourne, Australia: Monash University.

Advisory Committee on Human Rights and Foreign Policy (ACM), (29 May 1991). *Human Rights and International Economic Relations.* (Report No. 12; A12.A3V12). The Hague: ACM, PO Box 20061, 2500 EB The Hague.

Alston, Philip, Ed. (1996). *Human Rights Law.* New York: New York University Press.

Al-Attas, Syed Naguib (1993). *Some Aspects of Sufism as Understood and Practised Among the Malays.* Kuala Lumpur: Malaysian Sociological Research Institute (MSRI).

Augustine, Saint (1984). *The City of God.* London: Penguin Books.

Baehr, Peter R. (1999). *Universality in Practice.* New York: St. Martin's Press.

Baehr, Peter *et al.*, Eds. (1995). *Human Rights in Developing Countries: Yearbook 1995.* The Hague: Kluwer Law International.

Baldwin, David A. (1985). *Economic Statecraft.* Princeton, NJ: Princeton University Press.

Bangkok NGO Declaration on Human Rights (7 March 1993). Bangkok, Thailand.

Brady, J.D., 'Utility of Economic Sanctions as a Policy Instrument', in D. Leyton-Brown (1987). *The Utility of International Economic Sanctions.* New York: St. Martin's Press.

Bronkhorst, Daan and Gemma Crijns (2000). *Corporate Approaches: Human Rights and Business.* Amsterdam: Amnesty International (unpublished).

Bronkhorst, Daan (1995). *Truth and Reconciliation: Obstacles and Opportunities for Human Rights.* Amsterdam: Amnesty International.

Brown, C.C. (1952). *The Malay Annals, or Sejarah Melayu.* Oxford: Oxford University Press.

Catholic Bishops US, 'The Challenge of Peace: God's Promise and our Response: The Pastoral Letter on War and Peace', in Jean Bethke Elshtain, Ed. (1992). *Just War Theory.* New York: New York University Press.

Center for Economic and Social Rights (CESR), (1996). *UN Sanctions Suffering: A Human Rights Assessment of United Nations Sanctions on Iraq.*

Chaudhuri, K.N. (1990). *Asia before Europe: Economy and Civilisation of the Indian Ocean from the Rise of Islam to 1750.* Cambridge/New York: Cambridge University Press.

Christiansen, Drew and G.F. Powers, 'Economic Sanctions and the Just War Doctrine', in David Cortright and George A. Lopez, Eds. (1995). *Economic Sanctions: Panacea or Peacebuilding in a post-Cold War World?* Boulder, CO: Westview Press.

Clawson, Patrick (1993), 'Sanctions as Punishment, Enforcement, and Prelude to Further Action', in *Ethics and International Affairs,* Vol. 7.

Cortright, David and George A. Lopez, Eds. (1995). *Economic Sanctions: Panacea or Peacebuilding in a post-Cold War World?.* Boulder, CO: Westview Press.

Council of the European Community. *Resolution of the Council and of the Member States Meeting in the Council on Human Rights, Democracy and Development,* 1538th Council Meeting Development Co-operation, Brussels, 28 November 1991, 9555/91 (Presse 217-G).

Davis, Colin (1997). *Levinas: An Introduction.* Notre Dame, IN: University of Notre Dame Press.

Davis, Michael C., Ed. (1995). *Human Rights and Chinese Values: Legal, Philosophical, and Political Perspectives.* Hong Kong/New York: Oxford University Press.

Duparc, Christiane (1993). *The European Community and Human Rights.* Luxembourg: Office for Official Publications of the European Communities.

Dutch Interchurch Aid (1992). *Protocol on the Right to Humanitarian Assistance.* Utrecht, Netherlands: Stichting Oecumenische Hulp (SOH).

Elshtain, Jean Bethke, Ed. (1992). *Just War Theory*. New York: New York University Press.

European Commission, Directorate General for Development. *Report on the Implementation in 1994 of the Resolution of the Council and the Member States Meeting in the Council on Human Rights, Democracy and Development, adopted on 28 November 1991*, Brussels, VIII/1406/95-EN.

European Commission, *Directorate General for Development. Report on the Implementation in 1995 of the Resolution of the Council and the Member States Meeting in the Council on Human Rights, Democracy and Development, adopted on 28 November 1991*, Brussels, VIII/4.

European Parliament, The (1995). 'The World Trade Organization and the European Community', Working Paper of the European Parliament. Luxembourg.

Fairbank, John King, *et al.* (1976/1989). *East Asia: Tradition and Transformation.* Boston: Houghton Mifflin (published previously by Allen and Unwin, London, 1973).

Fisler Damrosch, Lori (1994), 'The Collective Enforcement of International Norms through Economic Sanctions', in *Ethics and International Affairs*, Vol. 8, No. 60.

Fuss, Diana (1989). *Essentially Speaking: Feminism, Nature and Difference.* New York: Routledge.

Genugten, W.J.M. van (1997). *WTO, ILO en EG: handelen in vrijheid.* Deventer: Tjeenk Willink.

Genugten, W.J.M. van, 'Universele gelding van mensenrechten en (de grenzen aan) het recht van bemoeienis van de internationale gemeenschap', in Y. Broer *et al.*, Eds. (1995). *Mensenrechten in Zuidoost-Azië: geijkte machteloosheid of nieuw beleid* (proceedings from the symposium of the same name). Utrecht.

Genugten, W.J.M. van (1996). 'Toelating tot de Raad van Europa: "acquis" op de tocht of gepaste rekkelijkheid?', in *Nederlands Juristenblad*, No. 7.

Genugten, W.J.M. van, and Gerard A. de Groot, Eds. (1999b). *United Nations Sanctions: Effectiveness and Effects, Especially in the Field of Human Rights; A Multi-disciplinary Approach.* Antwerpen; Groningen: Intersentia.

Ghai, Yash. (November 1994). *Human Rights and Governance: The Asian Debate* (Occasional Paper Series No. 1). California: The Asian Foundation's Center for Asian Pacific Affairs.

Gray, John, 'After the New Liberalism'. *Social Research*, New York, Vol. 61 (Fall 1994), No. 3.

Hauerwas, Stanley, 'On Surviving Justly: Ethics and Nuclear Disarmament', in Jean Bethke Elshtain, Ed. (1992). *Just War Theory*. New York: New York University Press.

Hauerwas, Stanley, 'A Pacifist Response to the Bishops', in Paul Ramsey (1988). *Speak up for Just War or Pacifism: A Critique of the United Methodist Bishops' Pastoral Letter 'In defense of Creation'.* University Park, PA: Pennsylvania State University Press.

Hayner, Priscilla B. (2000). *Unspeakable Truths: Confronting State Terror and Atrocities.* New York: Routledge.

Hazelzet, Hadewych A. (1996), *The Price of Morality in International Trade: Towards a Just Trade Theory.* Chicago, IL: University of Chicago, Committee on International Relations (ms).

Hazelzet, Hadewych A. (1997), 'Het prijskaartje van ethisch verantwoorde handel', in *Internationale Spectator*, The Hague, Vol. 2, No. 51.

Hazelzet, Hadewych, 'Assessing the Suffering from "Succesful" Sanctions: An Ethical Approach', in W.J.M. van Genugten and Gerard A. de Groot, Eds. (1999b). *United Nations Sanctions: Effectiveness and Effects, Especially in the Field of Human Rights; A Multi-disciplinary Approach.* Antwerpen; Groningen: Intersentia.

Holmes, Robert L. (1989). *On War and Morality.* Princeton, NJ: Princeton University Press.

Howard, Rhoda, 'Dignity, Community and Human Rights', in John Witte and Johan D. van der Vyver, Eds. (1996c). *Religious Human Rights in Global Perspective: Legal Perspectives.* The Hague: Martinus Nijhoff.

Hufbauer, Gary Clyde, Jeffrey J. Schott, Kimberly Ann Elliott (1985). *Economic Sanctions Reconsidered: History and Current Policy.* Washington DC: Institute for International Economics.

Huntington, Samuel P. (1991). *The Third Wave: Democratization in the Late Twentieth Century*. Norman: University of Oklahoma Press.

Information Office, the State Council of the People's Republic of China, 'Human Rights in China'. *Beijing Review*, Beijing, China, Vol. 34 (4-10 November 1991), No. 44.

Information Office, the State Council of the People's Republic of China, 'The Progress of Human Rights in China', *China Daily*, Beijing, China, 28 December 1995.

Al-Jauhari, Bukhair (Buchara) (1603). *Taj-us Salatin*. Edited by Khalid Hussain (1966). Kuala Lumpur: Dewan Bahasa dan Pustaka.

Johnson, James Turner, 'Threats, Values, and Defense: Does the Defense of Values by Force Remain a Moral Possibility?', in Jean Bethke Elshtain, Ed. (1992). *Just War Theory*. New York: New York University Press.

Kamminga, Menno Tjeerd (1990). *Inter-State Accountability for Violations of Human Rights* (dissertation). Leiden: University of Leiden.

Klaauw, A.W. van der (1997), 'Mensenrechten en ontwikkelingsbeleid van de Europese Gemeenschap', in *NJCM Bulletin*, 22, 10.

Lauren, Paul Gordon (1998). *The Evolution of International Human Rights: Visions Seen*. Philadelphia: University of Pennsylvania Press.

Leyton-Brown, D. (1987). *The Utility of International Economic Sanctions*. New York: St. Martin's Press.

Licht, Sonja, 'The Use of Sanctions in Former Yugoslavia: Can They Assist in Conflict Resolution?', in David Cortright and George A. Lopez, Eds. (1995). *Economic Sanctions: Panacea or Peacebuilding in a post-Cold War World?* Boulder, CO: Westview Press.

Lopez, George A. and David Cortright, 'Economic Sanctions in Contemporary Global Relations', in David Cortright and George A. Lopez, Eds. (1995). *Economic Sanctions: Panacea or Peacebuilding in a post-Cold War World?* Boulder, CO: Westview Press.

Luijk, Henk van (1993). *Om redelijk gewin. Oefeningen in bedrijfsethiek*. Amsterdam: Boom.

Martin, Lisa L. (1992). *Coercive Cooperation: Explaining Multilateral Economic Sanctions*. Princeton, NJ: Princeton University Press.

Meron, Theodor, Ed. (1985). *Human Rights in International Law: Legal and Policy Issues*. Oxford: Clarendon Press.

Milner, A.C., 'Islam and Malay Kingship', in Ahmad Ibrahim, Sharon Siddique, Yasmin Hussain, Eds. (1985). *Readings on Islam in Southeast Asia*. Singapore: Institute of Southeast Asian Studies.

Ministry of Foreign Affairs (September 1995). *De herijking van het buitenlands beleid*. (Dutch Government Proposal Redefining Foreign Policy). The Hague.

Mohamad, Goenawan (1994), 'Democracy', in *Sidelines: Writings from Tempo*. (Indonesia's weekly magazine, banned from 1994-1998). South Melbourne, Australia: Hyland House.

Mohamad, Goenawan (1994), 'Cocktail Parties', in *Sidelines: Writings from Tempo*. (Indonesia's weekly magazine, banned from 1994-1998). South Melbourne: Hyland House.

Morgenthau, Hans J., revised by Kenneth W. Thompson (c1993, 6th edn.). *Politics Among Nations: The Struggle for Power and Peace*. New York: McGraw-Hill.

Morsink, Johannes (1999). *The Universal Declaration of Human Rights. Origins, Drafting, and Intent*. Philadelphia: University of Pennsylvania Press.

Mukti Ali, A. (1970). *The Spread of Islam in Indonesia*. Yogyakarta, Indonesia: Jajasan NIDA.

Muzaffar, Chandra (1979). *Protector? An Analysis of the Concept and Practise of Loyalty in Leader-led Relationships within Malay Society*. Penang: Aliran Press.

An-Na'im, Abdullahi Ahmed, 'Towards a Cross-Cultural Approach to Defining International Standards of Human Rights', in Abdullahi Ahmed An-Na'im, Ed. (1992). *Human Rights in Cross-Cultural Perspectives: A Quest for Consensus*. Philadelphia: University of Pennsylvania Press.

An-Na'im, Abdullahi Ahmed et al. (1995). *Human Rights and Religious Values: An Uneasy Relationship?* Amsterdam: Rodopi.

Napoli, Daniela, 'The European Union's Foreign Policy and Human Rights', in Nanette A. Neuwahl and Allan Rosas, Eds. (1995). *The European Union and Human Rights*. The Hague: Kluwer Law International.

Netherlands Institute of Human Rights (SIM) (1989), 'The Universal Declaration of Human Rights: Its Significance in 1988', in *SIM*

Special, No. 9. Utrecht.

Ngobi, James C., 'The United Nations Experience with Sanctions', in David Cortright and George A. Lopez, Eds. (1995). *Economic Sanctions: Panacea or Peacebuilding in a post-Cold War World?* Boulder, CO: Westview Press.

Nincic, Miroslav and Peter Wallensteen (1983). *Dilemmas of Economic Coercion: Sanctions in World Politics.* New York: Praeger Publishers.

OECD (1996). *Trade, Employment and Labour Standards: A Study of Core Workers' Rights and International Trade.* Paris.

Oishi, Mikio (1997). *Aung San Suu Kyi's Struggle: Its Principles and Strategy* (JUST-Monograph). Penang, Malaysia: JUST World Trust.

Pigeaud, Theodore G.Th. (1960). *Java in the 14th Century: A Study in Cultural History.* The Hague: Martinus Nijhoff.

Poole, Hillary, Ed. (1999). *Human Rights: The Essential Reference.* Phoenix: Oryx Press.

Ramcharan, B.G., Ed. (1979). *Human Rights: Thirty Years After the Universal Declaration: Commemorative Volume on the Occasion of the Thirtieth Anniversary of the Universal Declaration of Human Rights.* The Hague: Martinus Nijhoff.

Ramsey, Paul, 'The Just War Doctrine According to Augustine', in Jean Bethke Elshtain, Ed. (1992). *Just War Theory.* New York: New York University Press.

Razak, Azizan Abdul (1980), 'The Law in Melaka Before and After the Coming of Islam', in *Tamadun Islam di Malaysia.* Kuala Lumpur: Persatuan Sejarah Malaysia (Malaysian History Society).

Rodley, Nigel S. (1985, 1999 2nd edn.). *The Treatment of Prisoners in International Law.* Oxford: Clarendon Press; New York: Oxford University Press.

Roosevelt, Eleanor (1961). *The Autobiography of Eleanor Roosevelt.* New York: Harper.

Rorty, Richard, 'Human Rights, Rationality, and Sentimentality', in Stephen Shule and Susan Hurley, Eds. (1993). *On Human Rights: The Oxford Amnesty Lectures 1993.* New York: Basic Books.

Rozemond, S., Ed. (1988). *Economische sancties.* The Hague: Nederlands Instituut voor Internationale Betrekkingen Clingendael.

Samnøy, Åshild (1993). *Human Rights as International Consensus: The Making of the Universal Declaration of Human Rights, 1945-1948.* Bergen, Norway: Chr. Michelsen Institute.

Schokkenbroek, J.G.C., 'De Margin of Appreciation-doctrine in de jurisprudentie van het Europese Hof', in A.W. Heringa, J.G.C. Schokkenbroek and J. van der Velde, Eds. (1990). *40 Jaar Europees Verdrag voor de Rechten van de Mens.* Leiden: NJCM.

Schrijver, Nico (1997). *Sovereignty over Natural Resources: Balancing Rights and Duties.* New York: Cambridge University Press.

Sen, Amartya, 'Our Culture, Their Culture'. in *The New Republic.* Washington, 1 April 1996.

SER (1996). *Sociaal-Economische Raad, Fundamentele arbeidsnormen en internationale handel.* The Hague.

Smith, Jacqueline, Ed. (1996). *Human Rights: Chinese and Dutch Perspectives.* The Hague: Martinus Nijhoff Publishers.

Tibbetts, G.R. (1971). *Arab Navigation in the Indian Ocean before the Coming of the Portuguese: Being a Translation of Kitab al-Fawa'id fi usul al-bahr wa'l-qawa'id of Ahmad ibn Majid al-Najdi.* London: Royal Asiatic Society of Great Britain and Ireland/Luzac Press.

Torres, R. (1996). 'Labour Standards and Trade', in *The OECD Observer*, 10-12.

Waley, Arthur (1939). *Three Ways of Thought in Ancient China.* London: Allen and Unwin.

Waltz, Kenneth N. (1979). *Theory of International Politics.* Reading MA: Addison Wesley.

Walzer, Michael (1977, 2nd edn. 1992). *Just and Unjust Wars: A Moral Argument with Historical Illustrations.* New York: Basic Books.

Watson Andaya, Barbara and Leonard Y. Andaya (1982). *A History of Malaysia.* London: MacMillan.

Werleigh, Claudette A., 'The Use of Sanctions in Haiti: Assessing the Economic Realities', in David Cortright and George A. Lopez, Eds. (1995). *Economic Sanctions: Panacea or Peacebuilding in a post-Cold War World?* Boulder, CO: Westview Press.

Woodward, Susan L., 'The use of Sanctions in Former Yugoslavia: Misunderstanding Political Realities', in David Cortright and George A. Lopez, Eds. (1995). *Economic Sanctions: Panacea or*

Peacebuilding in a post-Cold War World? Boulder, CO: Westview Press.

Yeo Cheow Tong (1997), 'Concluding Remarks by the Chairman: We have Delivered', in *WTO Focus*, No. 15, January 1997.

Zohar, Noam J. (1993), 'Boycott, Crime, and Sin: Ethical and Talmudic Responses to Injustice Abroad', in *Ethics and International Affairs*, Vol. 7.

The Humanist Committee on Human Rights (HOM)

The Netherlands Humanist Committee on Human Rights (Humanistisch Overleg Mensenrechten, HOM) is a non-governmental human rights organisation that is committed to strengthening the respect and the implementation of human rights in the broadest sense: universal, interdependent and indivisible.

Since its establishment in 1981 it has been the aim of the Netherlands Humanist Committee on Human Rights to stimulate public debate in the Netherlands and political improvements in human rights policies, to provide information on human rights issues and to support human rights activists abroad.

HOM gives special attention to gender and culture-related aspects. It is engaged in projects with the aim of raising awareness among specific target groups and carries out lobbying activities directed towards Dutch and European human rights policies. HOM is a participant in several Dutch and international networks on human rights.

Current HOM Projects

• *Women's Human Rights Project*
The gender discrimination of women is a violation of universal human rights and constitutes the leading motive in the Women's Human Rights Project. For a number of years the aims were to recognise and combat gender discrimination and violence against women in situations of conflict and women refugees. Currently the focus of HOM has switched to an awareness raising project concerning the importance of the UN Convention on the Elimination of All Forms of Discrimination against Women, with the publication of an informative booklet and several public meetings linked to the evaluation of the implementation of the Plan of Action of the UN Women's Conference in Beijing in 1995.

• *Linking Solidarity*
Since August 1995 HOM has been carrying out a project to support and to consolidate the work of organisations of relatives and friends of the 'disappeared'. 'Disappearances' occur in all continents, and relatives are kept in

uncertainty about the fate of their husband or son for years. In many countries all over the world they have established committees of relatives and other supportive groups. Apart from facilitating the exchange of experiences and knowledge, the aim is to give publicity to the work of these committees of relatives, and to explore ways and means of providing moral and material support. General information is available for any committee of this kind that wants to join the informal network in a written manual and by Internet. Much of the communication is now being exchanged by electronic mail.

• *Human Rights Impact Assessment*
In August 1999 HOM has started a new project: 'Universality and Conditionality: Developing a Human Rights Impact Assessment'. The project aims at the development of a human rights impact assessment framework and will contribute to the public debate on universality of human rights and on instruments for universal implementation, such as conditionality. The main focus of this impact assessment will initially be on human rights policies in foreign policies, but later on other international relations might be scrutinized also. The idea is to develop a set of indicators that will contribute to the analysis and impact of measures to combat and reduce human rights violations and to encourage the respect for human rights in different countries. Another part of this project is the publication of the English translation of articles on Asian and Western views on the value of human rights.

• *Human Rights Consultancy*
Activities are being expanded in the field of offering human rights expertise to related organisations, for example, providing courses, facilitating discussions, evaluating human rights projects. It is becoming increasingly clear that the human rights expertise of HOM has a valuable contribution to make to the activities of development organizations, training institutes and profit and non-profit enterprises. In these activities a cross-fertilisation is taking place between the activities in support of human rights organisations abroad, and awareness raising among the Dutch public.

The Netherlands Humanist Committee on Human Rights
P.O. Box 114
3500 AC Utrecht
The Netherlands
Tel. +31 30 233 40 27; Fax +31 30 236 71 04
E-mail: hom@hom.nl; Website: www.hom.nl